Effective Teaching in Today's *Classroom*

Integrating Technology into the Curriculum

2nd edition

Author
Kathleen Kopp
Foreword
Mike McQueen, M.L.I.S.

SHELL EDUCATION

Image Credits

p.58 svetlanarib/iStockphoto; p.167, 169 Kathleen Kopp; all other images Shutterstock

Shell Education

5301 Oceanus Drive
Huntington Beach, CA 92649-1030
http://www.shelleducation.com

ISBN 978-1-4258-1192-1

© 2015 Shell Educational Publishing, Inc.

Integrating Technology into the Curriculum

2nd edition

Table of Contents

Foreword

We all know the important role that technology plays in our students' current and future lives. They desperately need it to be competitive in the 21st century. Despite the fact that many students have been using technology since birth, they are constantly exposed to new high-tech environments, tools, and obstacles that challenge their prior experiences and influence their thinking as they progress into the future. The vast sea of technological possibilities, however, can be overwhelming for teachers, especially when trying to meet the many different needs of students.

As a teacher-librarian, one of the biggest, and most important professional responsibilities that I have is to help my colleagues integrate technology into their daily instruction. I know that many teachers are overloaded and overwhelmed with an exhausting list of demands on their already tight schedules. Far too often, teachers see technology as another "thing to do," instead of learning ways that technology can make their instruction easier and more effective.

Teachers need support and encouragement to keep up with the fast-paced world of technology, especially as innovation explodes throughout our world. Some school districts do a wonderful job of naturally embedding technology into their curriculum, but in most schools, this is not the case. Where can teachers turn to for help if their curriculum is missing practical advice or if professional support is not available? The answer: this book.

Throughout Integrating Technology into the Curriculum, 2nd edition, Kathleen Kopp seamlessly connects a wide range of instructional standards with lessons and planning. She carefully addresses the important role of the national technology standards developed by ISTE (International Society for Technology in Education). These standards are the foundational guidelines that thousands of schools nationwide rely on, to ensure that both students and staff head in the right direction in utilizing technology to enhance student learning.

Students are inundated with information every day and they need help developing skills to "identify, locate, evaluate, and effectively use the information they find as it relates to an issue or problem" (69). Because of my professional background, Chapter 3, "Technology to Support Literacy Instruction in English Language Arts," has a special place in my heart. I greatly appreciate the "Information Literacy" section, as these skills are the foundation of what our students need each and every day. The wide variety of examples and techniques provided entice teachers to dive in immediately with their students.

Flipped classrooms and online learning environments continue to explode in education. Many educators, however, struggle with ways to effectively balance a virtual learning environment with a face-to-face one. The insights, background information, tools, and resources in Chapter 5, "Online Applications to Extend Learning and Thinking," are very helpful to technology adapters of all levels, from beginner to advanced.

The tips, tools, and techniques that Kathleen Kopp provides will help teachers create 21st century lesson plans that will keep students on the right path for their technology-rich future. This book is worth reading, from cover to cover, or by jumping to whichever chapters address your most pressing needs. Enjoy!

Mike McQueen
M.L.I.S.
Teacher-Librarian, Author, and Speaker
Author of *Getting Boys to Read: Quick Tips for Parents and Teachers*
www.MikeMcQueen.com

Acknowledgments

I remember my first experience with computers, the good ol' Apple IIe. Alas, a new literacy station was born. I even participated in an online collaborative activity, what by today's standards would be called a STEM activity (Science, Technology, Engineering, and Mathematics). We compared the numbers and types of pets our students had at home. (Note: We were a rural school.) We analyzed how our pets compared to students who lived in suburban and urban settings. Urban homes had lots of fish. Rural ones had lots of horses. Don't ask me how I sent and received data; somehow, it just worked when I followed the directions.

At that time, there were no "technology specialists." No one was designated to support teachers with the integration of technology let alone to oversee the daily workings of the technology itself. Teachers were completely at a loss as to what to do with these new instructional tools; so usually they sat lifeless, taking up valuable counter or table space, or students played games on them when they were finished with their work.

Computers and technology have come so far since then. I am always willing to try the technology resources available to me. I value and appreciate my fellow teachers' attempts to do the same. We have so much to learn from one another. The added support of a technology teacher in our district's schools ensures that the technology I want to use works when I want it to. One such person, Bart Adams, is my go-to IT (information technology) guy for anything and everything in school and beyond. Presently, my school district is moving toward one-to-one integration. As I travel the state for various conferences and conventions, I stand before my colleagues perplexed at the lack of technology other schools and school districts offer their faculties and students. How can they possibly prepare students for the jobs of tomorrow when their schools don't have the technologies of today? I have a renewed appreciation for the efforts of my school district, under the leadership of Dr. Mike Geddes, to keep us current not just with regard to hardware but also with the instructional integration of technology for the advancement of student knowledge and 21st Century skills.

Of course, where would I be without my family? Thank you to my husband, Jeff. He is my live-in IT guy. Anytime the buttons I push don't respond accordingly, he always has a solution. (When he doesn't, we can always call Bart.)

I thank all the dedicated professionals out there, both near and far, who continue to provide meaningful and relevant technology integration ideas. There is a lot of information available to teachers and parents, if only we know where to look. Hopefully, the ideas in this book will inspire more reluctant teachers to stand bravely and push that button.

Introduction

What is new in education? Everything. This is especially true for the arena of educational technology. It has made its way into classrooms across the United States. One cannot pick up a professional journal without finding a connection to technology. Here are a few headlines taken from the U.S. News and World Report Education section of their website:

- "Study: Emerging Technology Has Positive Impact in Classroom"
- "More High Schools Implement iPad Program"
- "5 Unique Uses of Twitter in the Classroom"
- "LinkedIn Offers New Options for Students"

Technology means many things to many people. For some, it may mean computers and anything electronic. For others, it may mean any equipment necessary for any purpose. Teachers have been using technology in classrooms for many, many years. Recent advances have provided immeasurable support of instructional practices related to teaching and learning. This book provides any teacher in any teaching situation ideas for tools, techniques, strategies, and methods to readily and easily integrate technology into the curriculum for the expressed purpose of advancing student knowledge and personal growth.

On the other hand, today's technology is not without its challenges, especially for educators. This book attempts to help teachers overcome those challenges and the obstacles they may face enabling them to integrate technology into their lessons to maximize student learning and streamline their instructional planning, feedback, and assessment time.

Over the years there have been many pieces of technology available to teachers, such as the overhead projector, laminators, copy machines, and even multi-colored pens. The goal was and still is to use any available tool as a means to securing a specific student outcome. Often these technological tools motivate students to quickly become engaged with the lesson and allow them to maintain their enthusiasm throughout the learning process. This excitement is carried throughout the book as each idea is presented and explained.

As new technologies become available, it is thrilling to not only learn about them but to try them out with students. Some accomplish what was hoped; others fall far short. The former tend to be incorporated regularly into classroom routines and practices. The latter are discarded, not wanting to waste time "trying to make it work" just because the teacher next door loves it. Each of us has a unique style, set of comfort levels, and ways of doing things. The ideas in this book are intended to provide a smorgasbord of suggestions so that everyone can find something to implement right away. With the value and emphasis placed on technology in today's society, teachers, regardless of their own propensity for technology integration, owe it to their students to do all that they can to develop and strengthen their use of technology in the development of lessons and of student application of skills.

Technology today serves to ease the burdens teachers face throughout the school year as well as to enhance student learning and expand educational opportunities for them. We only need to embrace it and provide students with the necessary tools. This generation of students knows a lot about technology. They were born using it. It's time for schools to get on board, expand their repertoire of technology-related practices, and discover all the wonder that technology can bring to today's classrooms. This book will inspire you to explore options you may otherwise have only dreamed about.

Chapter 1

Today's Technology for Tomorrow's Classrooms

"Technology has forever changed not only what we need to learn, but the way we learn." —International Society for Technology in Education 2012, Standards

What is the go-to source for educators looking to maximize their technology instruction and use in the classroom? The answer is simple: ISTE. The International Society for Technology in Education (ISTE) is a membership association for educators who want to advance excellence in teaching and learning through the effective use of technology. This association provides resources for teachers, administrators, and all stakeholders in education, similar to how the International Reading Association (IRA), the National Council of Teachers of Mathematics (NCTM), and the National Science Teachers Association (NSTA) advance teaching practices with the goal of improving reading, math, and science achievement, respectively. ISTE houses information related to technology standards, offers professional development through conferences and publications, and connects educators from around the globe. However, its main focus is not the technology itself, but its resources to examine how teachers can use technology effectively to support instruction and learning.

ISTE specializes in taking technology that has arrived in classrooms and showing educators how to implement it so students' critical thinking and analysis skills are utilized. An example of this is the availability and use of a set of graphing calculators. These variable tools go beyond their obvious use: calculating complex (or even simple) algorithms and graphing the results. Although students may use this type of technology for its obvious intended purpose, these resources can go underutilized if teachers are unaware of all of their functions. Teachers can encourage students to collaborate to match a distance-time graph using a CBR (motion detector) attachment or compare the effects of chemicals in liquids using a thermometer attachment. Students can also use this technology to help them gather scientific data, organize it, and display it as part of a scientific exploration.

These advanced technology tools go beyond the mathematics classroom and can open a world of discovery and application in the science classroom as well. Yes, students need to learn how to solve and graph advanced algorithms. However, they also need to learn how to use technology as a tool to discover the relationships between events, think critically and analytically, solve real-world problems, and complete original projects. These are the skills 21st century students need to be successful in today's technologically advanced society. These are the skills and applied practices teachers must provide students so that they can successfully compete in a technologically advanced global society.

Looking Back on Technology

Imagine how excited people were to be able to dial a few numbers and talk with others—family, friends, co-workers—across great distances. The telephone allowed this to happen. Before the introduction of the telephone, imagine how grateful people were to be able to quickly send messages, transmitted as signals, over land and sea. The telegraph enabled this to happen. But before that, people could share the written word with greater ease thanks to the printing press, which reduced the need for handwritten communications. Now, imagine walking into an abandoned cave and "reading" the messages left behind by the previous occupants. Prehistoric tools created the etchings archaeologists and anthropologists still study today, gaining insight into our ancestors' earliest attempts at communication. If schools existed back then, we imagine students bringing stone tablets, rocks, and picks to class with which to record their thoughts and demonstrate their understanding.

Schools have come a long way since the Stone Age. Even schools which by today's standards might seem to have "limited technology" have experienced some of its benefits throughout the years.

The overhead projector made its debut in the 1930s, having been initially used by the military for training purposes (http://www.edudemic.com/classroom-technology/). It eventually morphed into a useful instructional tool by teachers in schools. It allowed educators to face and engage in conversations with students directly, rather than turning their backs to record thoughts, ideas, or assignments on the board.

In a blog posted by Larry Cuban, he reminisces over what was available to 1950s teachers. He specifically mentions the use of the ditto machine, "Ah, just typing in the phrase brings back memories of smelling alcohol and purple stained fingers from handling those 'spirit masters' " (2013); along with film strip and 16mm film projectors. These technologies saw many decades of hard use, bringing unlimited handouts to students and providing teachers with just enough leverage to keep students engaged; after all, only one lucky classmate would be chosen to turn the film from slide to slide.

Common recent practice had students engaged exclusively in paper-pencil tasks, such as accessing literature and information through textbooks, writing summaries on notebook paper, and completing math exercises on activity pages. However, our digital world is quickly overtaking our traditional paper-pencil world. All of the tools just discussed are being replaced by modern-day technological advancements. These tools, such as electronic documents and direct audio-video access, allow teachers to expand learning beyond the four classroom walls and engage students in creative communications, all with the touch of just a few buttons.

The Digital Age in the Classroom

Today's technologically advanced classrooms have a host of digital components that are now becoming commonplace in the education world. Computer stations, portable computer labs, electronic equipment (e.g., digital microscopes) and measurement devices (e.g., digital balance scales), mounted projectors, document cameras, interactive whiteboards, tablets, and eReaders are just some of the tools today's students use in the classroom. With all of this technology at the ready, how does a classroom in today's digital age look?

Reading: Podcasts Enhance Fluency

According to the Reading Rockets website, "Fluency is the ability to read a text accurately, quickly, and with expression. Fluency is important because it provides a bridge between word recognition and comprehension" (2014, "Reading 101 - Fluency"). When students read fluently, they read words automatically, which facilitates comprehension.

An effective means of helping students improve their reading fluency is to use reader's theater scripts. These are texts written in the format of a play, with each character having his or her part. There may or may not be a narrator, but scripts typically include stage directions. Research has shown that this method of rehearsed reading practice leads to improved reading fluency (sight word recognition, quick and accurate decoding, the application of appropriate phrasing, and the acknowledgment of punctuation), as well as an increased interest in reading (Griffith and Rasinski 2004; Young and Rasinski 2009). Consequently, as readers become more fluent, they are able to increase their comprehension, as they expend less energy in the actual decoding process and more energy in the comprehension process (Pikulski and Chard 2005).

In years past, teachers would print adequate copies of the reader's theater script for students using it in small groups. Students would read and reread the text, conveying meaning through verbal inflection, facial expressions, and actions. While there is a lot of value in this, today's digital-age students have the added benefits of technology. Digital tools cannot only promote motivation and engagement but also help educators differentiate instruction for their students by "scaffold[ing] learning environments where support can be adjusted in relation to students' needs and preferences" (Dalton 2008, 155). One such tool is a podcast.

In the context of reader's theater, they can be used as recitals where students record their rehearsed parts and post their work as a podcast online. In a ten-week reader's theater podcasting study that included repeated reading, recording, podcasting, and listening to the published audio, struggling second- and third-grade students averaged a gain of 1.3 years in reading comprehension (Vasinda and McLeod 2011). With the integration of podcasting to enhance an already research-based effective strategy for improving reading, "Both students and teachers noted the wider audience, the permanency, and also alluded to audio as a visualizing medium" (Vasinda and McLeod 2011, 489).

> A *podcast* is a digital audio file that is first uploaded to and then can be downloaded from a website to a media player or computer. These types of recordings are generally used as tutorials or lectures.

Writing: Automated Essay-Scoring Programs Enhance the Writing Process

One of the challenges teachers face when assigning written work is grading all of it in a timely and personalized manner. Automated systems are growing in popularity because they can produce scores more reliably, quickly, and at a lower cost than human scoring (Topol, Olson, and Roeber 2011). Providing essential and timely feedback to students is crucial in our quest to maximize student learning. One tool to employ is taking advantage of the digitally enhanced classroom. Students can type stories, essays, and reports into automated scoring programs and receive immediate feedback as they continue to craft their writing. These automated scoring systems are based in natural language processes. They apply the principles of linguistics to computer science, creating a system that interacts with human language, both spoken and written. This technology has been recently scrutinized due to advancements in computerized testing that include written (typed) responses. The Educational Testing Service (ETS) supports the use of automated scoring systems, citing five essential ideas when considering the use of such systems (2013).

ETS contends that automated scores

- are consistent with human scores;
- are understandable and meaningful;
- are fair;
- are valid; and
- can impact the reported scores of the overall test.

With the use of embedded spelling and grammar checking features in word-processing programs, students in today's classrooms have few excuses for submitting documents with misspelled words and incorrect grammar. This minor enhancement to the writing process can, at the very least, assist with students' writing fluency, so teachers can focus on grading content as opposed to conventions.

Online Essay Scoring Resources

Students who might take the Test of English as a Foreign Language (TOEFL) or the Scholastic Aptitude Test (SAT) are able to use online practice tests that include electronically scored written components that serve to improve their time management skills and to gain competency and confidence with the testing format (Encomium Online, www.encomiuminteractive.com/exams/products_details.asp?egid=3).

Math: Handheld Devices Help Students Learn to Tell Time

Do you remember manipulating or having your students manipulate a paper clock to learn how to tell time? Any time or elapsed time could be modeled and practiced (e.g., hour, half-hour, quarter-hour, five-minute intervals) using these clocks. Today, in the digital classroom, students who have the advantage of using smartphones, tablets, or individual computers can use apps, such as MiniSchool, Todo Telling Time, and Tic Toc Time, to learn to tell time and calculate elapsed time. With a touch of the screen, the minute and/or hour hand moves around the digital clock face. When students select a button, the device announces the time shown on the clock. Additionally, students can take quizzes, play games, and otherwise learn to tell time through interactive activities, thanks to today's technology.

A Rationale for Technology Integration: Into the Future

What tomorrow's technology brings to teachers and students is limited only by our imaginations. What is clear is that today's students are part of the digital era. Teachers can assume that a majority (upward of three-fourths) of the children entering their classrooms have been

> Technology can effectively enhance any school subject, such as science, social studies, health, media, music, and art. Chapters 3 and 4 provide specific and effective suggestions for technology integration in English language arts and the content areas.

exposed to computers and the Internet since they were infants. According to the United States Census Bureau (2013), the percentage of households with computers rose from just over half (56.3 percent) in 2001 to 75.6 percent in 2011; and the percentage of households that use the Internet rose from 50.4 percent to 71.7 percent. As more students become connected at home, they may come to expect to be connected at school.

Learning through digital media is a real and familiar delivery system for our students. While students use flat-screen computers, tablets, and smartphones today, they may use three-dimensional holographic images tomorrow. Even though teachers use copiers to print papers or documents today, they may use three-dimensional printers in the near future for a host of new purposes. Albeit robotics are a thing of the movies today, they may find their way into tomorrow's schools to benefit students, teachers, administrators, and support staff with instructional applications, learning opportunities, management systems, or quality care (i.e., automated lunchrooms, clinic assistance, or disciplinary actions). With advances in technology comes a requirement for people to continually revisit their moral and ethical positions regarding related controversial topics, such as genetic engineering. Will educational institutions and instructional leaders be ready?

The future of what technology might offer schools is exciting, but it could leave some educators feeling uneasy or skeptical. Unfortunately, for all of the technology available, schools tend to lag behind in shifting instruction to meet the demands of society. Teachers can no longer use computers for rote skill practice or for low-level instructional assignments and believe that they are effectively integrating technology into the curriculum. According to the Partnership for 21st Century Skills (2013), learners must be engaged in critical, analytical tasks. They must learn to solve problems and work collaboratively. The Partnership has organized a system of essential skills into what they refer to as the *Four Cs*: critical thinking, communication, collaboration, and creativity. The organization has proposed student outcomes related to core subjects, such as reading and math; learning and innovation; life and career; and information, media, and technology. The latter set of skills is closely linked, since much of the information students receive and the media they use is connected in some way to technology. Even so, they each hold their own set of skills necessary for success in school and in life. Information literacy refers to students' abilities to access and evaluate information. Media literacy refers to students' abilities to analyze media and technology skills (oftentimes referred to as ICT, information and communication technology). It also refers to students' abilities to use and apply technology effectively (for research, organization, and communication) and ethically.

> People in the 21st century live in a technology- and media-suffused environment, marked by various characteristics, including 1) access to an abundance of information, 2) rapid changes in technology tools, and 3) the ability to collaborate and make individual contributions on an unprecedented scale. To be effective in the 21st century, citizens and workers must be able to exhibit a range of functional and critical thinking skills related to information, media, and technology. (Partnership for 21st Century Skills 2013, under "A Vision for 21st Century Citizenship")

Technology and 21st-century skills are inextricably linked in today's classrooms. However, educators may ask what this looks like. These ideas are explored closely through the following examples. Although these examples are structured uniquely for each criterion, readers should identify overlap among the Four Cs.

Technology for the Advancement of Critical Thinking

Critical thinking skills include being able to analyze, argue logically, justify, and evaluate. Students who exhibit critical thinking skills ask questions, seek answers, and strive to rationalize thoughts and ideas to help make sense of the world around them. Typically, the types of activities that require the use of critical-thinking skills are high on Bloom's taxonomy (Vanderbilt University 2014). In order for students to think critically, they must participate in open-ended activities that challenge what they know and require them to apply problem-solving skills in unique and original contexts. Wendy Conklin (2012) reminds teachers that classrooms that encourage critical thinking emphasize learning as well as knowing. For example, a student who knows the equation to find the volume of a geometric solid but cannot use this information to determine the possible dimensions of a 24-cubic-foot refrigerator has not really *learned* this concept, even though he or she *knows* it. Critical thinking is not a new idea in education; however, the purposeful use of technology opens an entirely new world to teachers and students as they analyze, question, and construct learning. In this regard, technology is a tool for developing critical thinking skills.

To help students build this type of thinking, teachers can have students

- evaluate a website for its validity, reliability, and accuracy;

- compare two or more websites on one topic, and identify one site as more useful than the other(s), citing reasons;

- use an online simulation to reason abstractly; and

- use online research to find facts, information, and statistics about a controversial subject; align with one side; and use the information to support a position.

Technology for the Advancement of Communication

As detailed in the "Classroom Snapshot: Looking Back on Technology" section earlier in this chapter, people have been inventing new and improved ways to communicate throughout time. Today's technology enables us to communicate with each other virtually through emailing, texting, chatting (typing in a chat room), blogging, posting (to a social network), and video chatting. Gamers, people who play video or computer games, can even talk to each other through their gaming systems when they are connected to the Internet. With a headset and a microphone, two or more gamers can spend the day together in virtual reality as if they were sitting side-by-side on the couch teaming up against zombies and warriors. Regardless of our preferred means of communication, technology is the means through which we communicate. It is the tool we use to share and exchange a thought or idea, information, or news.

Suggestions for teachers to offer effective integration of technology for the purpose of communication are as follows:

- Use a wiki or cloud-based storage option for students to collaborate on research projects.

- Have students post (tweet) summaries of assigned readings on Twitter.

- Set up a classroom webpage and have students author important information, such as vocabulary terms used in context, how-to summaries of math processes, and upcoming events.

Technology for the Advancement of Collaboration

People collaborate to accomplish all kinds of tasks. If we look closely, we will see evidence of collaboration in the grocery store, at the auto repair shop, at restaurants, with local emergency operations, such as police, fire, and paramedics, and pretty much in any career or summer job choice students might make.

Christopher Cattie and Kris van Riper (2012) summarized a Corporate Executive Board (CEB) survey of over 23,000 employees across industries and locations. They noted that the nature of collaboration has changed. More than two-thirds of employees reported that their jobs require more collaboration today than they did three years ago. Moreover, employee networks are expanding and becoming increasingly cross-functional. Sixty percent of respondents said their day-to-day work requires regular coordination with ten or more people, and two-thirds reported regular coordination with employees from different work units and supervisory levels (para. 2).

Collaboration is a skill that comes naturally and easily to some; for others, it must be taught. With technology being such an integral part of our everyday lives, teachers must attend to this critical *C* by employing strategies that integrate technology through a collaborative effort. The first suggestion under the previous *C*, communication, offered one way students may collaborate to accomplish a common goal. The following are a few other suggestions:

- Join a collaborative online project with other classrooms from around the world (e.g., Global SchoolNet or Cyberbee).

- Work as a small group to collect scientific data, and then organize it into a spreadsheet or graphing program to share with the class.

- Work with a partner to identify key words and ideas from a selected narrative or informative text, enter them into the Wordle website, and share the resulting organizer with the class to help identify themes or main ideas.

> A *Wordle* is a creative writing tool used to "show" prominent words in a text, discussion, or brainstorming session. Once typed or otherwise loaded in, it organizes the words into what is referred to as a "cloud of words," enlarging some and minimizing others based on their frequency of use.

Technology for the Advancement of Creativity

Most students like to be creative. Students are productive when they are allowed to design and create an original project related to a topic. To illustrate this point, with just one of many examples, Gregory Childress (2014) reported on a creative teenager at The School for Creative Studies in Durham, NC. This 6-12 magnet school's curriculum "focuses on digital media and creative design" ("Student of the Month"). One of their students, Mattiyah Jones, reflects on the positive feedback she receives from her creative talents. She says, "I came to this school because my mom knows I was creative. I like to make things, put things together and draw. [My mom] felt like it was a good fit for me and believed it's a school I will excel in" (Childress 2014).

Intentionally designed assignments have this advantage for students. Teachers can assess their students' levels of learning from basic knowledge and comprehension levels to the highest evaluation and synthesis levels. In exchange, students get to share their learning through more authentic tasks rather than rote paper-and-pencil worksheets, assignments, and tests. The value of creativity in the classroom is evidenced in what future employers require of their employees. Creativity leads to innovation. Innovation leads to economic growth. Economic growth leads to increased employment, and so on. In fact, Singapore and Korea emphasize creativity in their curricula from elementary school through secondary school (Vincent-Lancrin 2013). Heidi Hayes Jacobs (2010) advocates for curricula that nurtures creativity in all learners. Students can demonstrate creativity by participating in innovative and original tasks or by completing assignments that place students in open-ended problem-solving situations. With regard to technology, these ideas allow students to be creative and innovative thinkers while staying true to the subject matter required by state and national curricula. Some examples are:

- Use building block sets with motorized parts to design and create a vehicle to perform a certain function or complete a certain task.

- Use digital or multimedia options to design and create a book review.

- Use multimedia software to create an original quiz game centered on a particular content-area topic.

More Benefits of Integrated Technology

Technology has many benefits for teachers and students as indicated, particularly as a means to learn and apply the essential 21st-century learning skills of critical thinking, communication, collaboration, and creativity. Additionally, integrating technology into the curriculum can shift the responsibility of learning from the teacher to his or her students. David Nagel (2014) defines these teachers as ones who "routinely use digital strategies in their work with students and act as guides and mentors" ("Near-Term Shifts: Teaching and Learning with Tech"). As students access information digitally and complete instructional activities through technology, they become active participants in the learning process. Students are no longer restricted to working independently, returning to school the next day to turn in an assignment, and then waiting at least another day to receive their grade or what their teacher thought of it. For example, instead of sitting in class listening to their teacher teach and then having to work, students in the digital age can read informational text online, add notes or ideas as they read, summarize information using a text-based software program, and submit and receive feedback from their teacher electronically. In this situation, the teacher provides a direction for students by selecting links to the assigned reading material. Students, using their computers, do the rest. Through interactive communication devices, students can ask their teacher questions and receive immediate responses. Students can post their work to an electronic storage system, which the teacher can access and give feedback through, making this information available for students at any time.

Benefits for Students

The effective integration of technology can build more cohesive teacher-student and teacher-parent relationships and improve the academic achievement of students. Consider a group of second-grade teachers at Middleton Elementary School in Woodbury, Minnesota. On their website, Almost a Third Grader, they created a series of online learning videos to help their second graders transition into third grade. The site was intended for summer viewing, and students who watched the creative skits and narrations (some starring Gunner the dog) could review what they learned the previous school year and gain insights into the challenges they would face as third graders. Through digital media, these teachers not only demonstrated their commitment to teaching and learning, but they also addressed their students' concerns and/or apprehensions about the upcoming school year. Additionally, they strengthened teacher–parent connections. Parents could easily link to see what their children should know and get a glimpse of the adventurous learning to take place during the upcoming school year.

Benefits for Teachers

Teachers, too, benefit from the effective integration of technology into the curriculum. They improve their effectiveness in the classroom through informational sharing sites, such as Edmodo, Moodle, blogs, and wikis, which allow teachers to benefit from each other. For example, a teacher who is looking for a whiz-bang idea related to the skill of making inferences might find just what he or she seeks on an online educational forum. Additionally, teachers who frequent these sites improve their own information literacy skills, which better enables them to instruct their students in technology use. Some of these sites are specific to education. Others, such as Pinterest, are open to miscellaneous areas of interest. Some require accounts with login credentials, and some "groups" within them require passwords.

Benefits for Student Achievement

Finally, but arguably most importantly, effective technology integration can lead to improved student success and overall achievement across subject areas. Because "technology" is such a broad topic, research regarding its effectiveness with student achievement has been targeted to specific technology in specific instructional areas. For example, researchers have studied the effects of the use of interactive whiteboards in reading (Digregorio and Sobel-Lojeski 2009, 2010) and math (Linder 2012); the effects of using blogs, wikis, and podcasts (Richardson 2010); and the effects of using games or gamelike programs (Tuzun et al. 2009). All the same, past research demonstrates the positive effects that the integration of technology can have on learning (Hawkins 1997; White, Ringstaff, and Kelley 2002). Current research accepts several known facts about the use of technology in learning. According to Namsoo Shin et al. (2012), educational technology researchers already know that "technology and games have yielded consistently positive results with regard to motivation, persistence, curiosity, attention, and attitude toward learning" (540).

As with any instructional tool, technology is only effective in improving the academic achievement of students when it is used with purpose, meaning, and relevance. For example, a teacher who has and uses an electronic reading program is not guaranteed higher student achievement just because the program is the main instructional tools used in the classroom. Along with the use of the technology, the teacher must set clear instructional outcomes, deliver outstanding lessons, use research-based instructional strategies, closely monitor student engagement, continuously monitor student progress, and adjust instruction accordingly to best match students to materials and tasks. According to a study by CompTIA, the IT Industry Association (2011), teachers and school leaders believe that "technology has positively impacted the classroom and the productivity of students" and that "roughly 65 percent of educators also believe that students are more productive today than they were three years ago, due to the increased reliance on technology in the classroom" ("Making the Grade"). As technology continues to make its way into America's classrooms, teachers are learning how to use it with meaning, purpose, and as a supportive tool for overall effective instruction.

We recently studied eight secondary districts throughout the United States that exemplify the creative use of technology in K–12 schools, particularly what leaders in these schools did to make sure technology enhanced learning. For these districts, we found, using technology is not the goal. It never was. These schools achieved their results by focusing on learning-centered goals like making learning relevant, providing new opportunities to close achievement gaps, and improving graduation rates and college readiness. In other words, their goal was to educate students for work and life in the 21st century, not just to add technology. (Levin and Schrum 2013, 51)

Challenges for Educators

An article published by Education Week (Editorial Projects in Education Research Center 2011), lists several challenges schools face with regard to technology. First of all, technology advances rapidly. Schools and school districts do what they can to keep their technology fresh and current.

Teachers can use in class with students tomorrow only what they know exists today. When new technology comes tomorrow, teachers will devise a plan to use it the next day with their students; but by that time, tomorrow will be today, and something else new and exciting will have come along for teachers to use.

Secondly, this same article reports that with the rapid changes that occur with technology every day, teachers, administrators, students, and parents all face challenges with regard to its effective integration. "Longitudinal research that takes years to do risks being irrelevant by the time it is completed because of shifts in the technological landscape. The iPad, for instance, became popular in schools soon after it was released and well before any research could be conducted about its educational effectiveness" (2011, para. 4).

Just keeping up with what is fresh and current is a full-time job, and simply finding or finding out about technology is not enough. Teachers must effectively integrate technology to support, enhance, and extend learning and thinking. For example, teachers may have students use computers and presentation software to generate a report about a specific science or social studies topic. However, depending on the criteria the students must meet, this assignment can remain a very low-level comprehension task. In this instance, the computer and software just become digital paper and pencil. Although this type of assignment certainly has its place in today's schools, teachers who use computers and software only to have students complete tasks at a low level (such as simple research projects or drill exercises) are missing the greater scope of what technology has to offer teachers and students in today's classrooms.

With the wide range of options available, teachers might easily get wrapped up in technology for technology's sake and lose sight of the overall goal: to improve student learning. The previous example illustrates this point. Teachers are busy people. They want to engage students in meaningful work. As valuable a skill as report writing is, it likely does not challenge students to think critically or analytically, a necessary and essential part of today's learning environment. To effectively integrate technology for meaningful purposes, teachers can and should consider how the technology students use helps them develop any one or more of the 4 Cs of 21st-century skills discussed earlier in this chapter. For example, as eReaders become more popular and prevalent in today's classrooms, teachers will want to devise a plan for students to use them not only to practice reading, but also to apply critical thinking and communication skills. Perhaps students post a book review on a classroom website or access two informational texts on the same topic, comparing how each author chose to deliver the information and explain which text they preferred and why.

All of this talk about technology's impact on student learning is meaningless if schools are not adequately equipped with the hardware (computers) they need to achieve the greatest impact. Schools with multiple computer labs, portable labs, or independent student stations in classrooms have obvious benefits over schools where the only lucky individual to have access to a computer is the teacher. Additionally, the availability of LCD projectors, interactive whiteboards, document cameras, and audio and video feeds can directly impact the overall effectiveness of a teacher's ability to integrate technology into the curriculum. Schools and school districts needing to add, update, and/or expand their hardware supplies can seek grant funding opportunities, investigate fundraising options, and consider entering contests with technology equipment awards. These ideas are explored in more depth in the next section.

Schools with an adequate supply of hardware may face challenges over time with regard to system management. Twenty-five computers with outdated operating systems will not benefit students. Whether there is one computer in the classroom or several, schools can also run into connectivity challenges. There are limitations to a school's wide area network (WAN) and local area network (LAN). Either or both of these can affect a school's bandwidth, which can limit the amount of online learning students can access at one time. One option for improving student access to the Internet is to provide additional wireless connectivity through the use of a mobile hotspot generator. These devices are small, portable boxes that use a cellular network. They allow several wireless devices to access the Internet using a wireless boost.

> Some schools and school districts have strict policies regarding the use of external devices on school property. Teachers interested in using mobile hotspots to increase their students' access to the Internet should check with a school or district technology coordinator to learn of any limitations at their school.

Options for Financing Technology

Administrators and teachers interested in expanding their school's hardware, software, or connectivity have several options available to financially support this endeavor. First, grants provide opportunities for schools to develop a plan with regard to time, resources, materials, and people that best suit them, their student population, their teacher knowledge level with technology, and their community base. Knowing what a school wants and needs, and finding a grant to meet these needs, can take time and patience. Some grant applications are quite extensive and require quite a bit of preplanning and forethought to complete. Regardless, the benefits of receiving such grants can mean the world to students. Doing some background research on how to write and submit a good grant application is time well spent.

Grant-Writing Tips

School administrators and teachers interested in writing grants to fund technology should abide by the following simple tips:

- Read any and all information related to the grant. This includes who the money is intended for, what types of programs the grant supports, and guidelines and submission regulations. Do not skip anything. It helps, too, to read winning submissions from previous grants. Mimic these proposals with regard to format and content.

- Devise an innovative, creative, and original idea that is based, above all, on student achievement. Infuse research to support this project.

- Identify SMART goals (Doran, Miller, and Cunningham): Goals that are Specific, Measurable, Attainable, Relevant, and Timely.

- Projects that can be replicated sometimes gain points by the grant evaluators.

- Synthesize a detailed, itemized budget.

- Review the evaluation criteria. The proposal should address all the criteria and be written in clear, understandable language.

In addition to applying for grants, administrators and teachers can enter contests to win technology products for a school. Typically, companies that represent a specific product offer sweepstakes or contests where those who enter can win free products and services from the company. Before spending lots of money on interactive whiteboards, such as Mimios or iPads, schools should access these companies' websites and check to see if they are offering any special promotions or contests.

Outside of grants and contests, schools can participate in school-wide fundraising events. Bake sales, carnivals, book fairs, and private sales companies (which sell cookie dough, candy bars, paper products, or other miscellaneous materials) are just a few fundraising options. Also, schools can elicit the assistance of larger retailers to boost fundraising support. For example, schools can schedule a day and time with retailers so that a certain percentage of the sales made within that time frame comes back to the school. Similarly, schools can post projects, supply needs, or special event funding needs online for anonymous donations through such sites as DonorsChoose.org or GoFundMe.com. When engaging in fundraising, schools should have a plan for the use of the funds raised and clearly communicate this plan to parents and community members. Family and friends might be more willing to support a child's school if they know what the money is for and how it will benefit the school and community.

Finally, schools can look into recycling old hardware to gain devices and money for upgrading and replacing outdated equipment. Some schools have drop-off locations where parents and community members may donate their gently used digital devices, particularly smartphones that no longer have service contracts but still work and mini-tablets that can connect with any wireless network. Students will not be privileged with the latest and greatest hardware, but this program will put much-needed technology in the hands of students. In addition, many local communities have computer-recycling centers where people trade in their old technology equipment for cash. Furthermore, some computer retailers allow people to trade in their old equipment for discounts on new equipment. This may or may not be an option for schools or school districts depending on finance laws and regulations, but they are something to consider.

Conclusion

This chapter provided a few insights into the world of technology as it relates to teaching and learning in order to lay a foundation for the idea that effective technology integration is essential for students in today's classrooms. Regardless of their familiarity and comfort level with technology, teachers in all settings and situations should do what they can to move into the world of digital teaching and learning. Our students will grow to become even more reliant on technology in the future. The time is now for schools to ensure success for all in this digital age.

Reflect and Respond

1. In what ways do you integrate technology into your classroom?

2. Who benefits more from integrating technology into the classroom, teachers or students? Why?

3. When you look for ways to use technology, which 21st century skills do students apply most often?

4. How do you believe your students will respond to the use of more technology integration in their day-to-day learning?

Chapter 2

Technology and Curriculum Standards for Teachers and Students

Today's classrooms continue to focus on curriculum standards. States have been implementing their own instructional standards for language arts, math, science, social studies, health, physical education, and fine arts. States may have had technology standards, too, or these may have been embedded within the general content-area standards. Today, many states are implementing rigorous standards for English language arts, mathematics, science, and social studies. Accompanying these are digital assessments, requiring students to apply word-processing skills and to use basic digital functions, such as scrolling and drag-and-drop.

The world of instructional standards in education is complex, and today's instructional standards are directly linked to assessments. Some states, schools, and school districts may be using the national education standards, while others may not. The same is true with technology standards. Some states may not require the implementation of *any* technology standards, rather, they expect teachers to instruct students in applied technology skills that meet the national or state standards. In theory, attending to only these applied and integrated technology standards will increase students' likelihood of performing well on the digital national curriculum assessments. So, somewhere

> The first step for teachers is to know whether they are:
>
> - required to implement the national technology standards
> - required to implement the state technology standards
> - only required to implement the integration of technology through the Common Core State Standards
> - not required to implement any technology standards

along the way, teachers need to ensure that students are technologically (let alone instructionally) prepared to take these assessments.

For example, the East Windsor Public School District in Connecticut, on their website related to Departments and Programs, Information Technology, has this to say to their teachers regarding the Guiding Principles of Instructional Technology in K–12: *Technology should be used by students and teachers to facilitate learning. The content areas provide a curricular context for the use of technology. Classroom practice should reflect not only the National Education Technology Standards and profiles, but also the standards of the National Council of Teachers of Mathematics, the International Reading Association, and the National Council for the Social Studies. Technology is not to be promoted in isolation, but rather should be an integral tool for learning and communication within the context of academic subject areas.* (District Offices, Information Technology)

Teachers who have this information may more diligently and effectively prepare students to meet these expectations. At the very least, teachers have an obligation to ensure that students have the technology skills they need to attend to digital assessments with confidence. The following pages outline technology standards both as stand–alone standards and as integrated standards. A sample lesson plan details how teachers might tackle the standards they use.

National Technology Standards

The International Society for Technology in Education (ISTE) has developed its own standards for teaching and learning in today's digital age. According to the ISTE website, their standards are "widely recognized and adopted worldwide." Their standards are adopted by all 50 states and six countries. They are organized by standards for students, teachers, administrators, coaches, and computer science educators. They list the skills and knowledge each of these stakeholders needs to function digitally and globally.

ISTE-S (Students)

ISTE developed standards for students in 2007. According to the ISTE website (2012), "Simply being able to use technology is no longer enough. Today's students need to be able to use technology to analyze, learn, and explore. Digital-age skills are vital for preparing students to work, live, and contribute to the social and civic fabric of their communities." The ISTE-S are divided into six categories (www.iste.org/standards/standards-for-students):

- Communication and Collaboration
- Creativity and Innovation
- Critical Thinking, Problem Solving, and Decision Making
- Digital Citizenship
- Research and Information
- Technology Operations

Rather than having individual grade-level standards, these standards are general, overarching statements of what students should know and be able to do within each of these categories.

Examples of the Critical Thinking, Problem Solving, and Decision Making category are:

- Identify and define authentic problems and significant questions for investigation.

- Plan and manage activities to develop a solution.

- Collect and analyze data to identify solutions and/or make informed decisions.

- Use multiple processes and diverse perspectives to explore alternative solutions.

Teachers adapt each of these standards within their respective grade levels by designing well-constructed and meaningful lessons that take into consideration the students' age and general ability level. Figure 2.1 gives sample lesson suggestions across grade levels.

Figure 2.1 Sample Instructional Activities for Students to Think Critically, Problem Solve, and Make Decisions

Grades	Sample Instructional Activity
2–3	**Problem:** An ice cream truck owner wants to sell ice cream on the corner after school. The owner can hold only three different ice cream treats in her truck. She needs to know which ice cream treats the students at school like best in order to make the most sales.
	Task: Survey students, teachers, and parents. Run a graphing program to show the results of the survey. Then operate a publishing program to design and create a poster for the truck. Utilize the poster to advertise the items that will be for sale. Use creative vocabulary to entice would-be ice cream buyers to make a purchase.
5–6	**Problem:** Scientists are concerned about a local pond ecosystem. They worry that an overpopulation of algae is negatively affecting the balance of life in the pond.
	Task: Conduct research to uncover the biotic and abiotic factors that contribute to a pond ecosystem. Also, learn how algae can impact this ecosystem. Create a slide show presentation summarizing the biotic and abiotic factors that make up a balanced pond ecosystem. Include text and graphics, such as pictures and charts. Then explain how too much algae can impact this ecosystem. Include at least one likely cause for the increase in algae and what scientists might do to restore balance.
9–10	**Problem:** A local energy company wants to build a power substation near protected land. Local ecologists are concerned that this will negatively impact plant and animal life in the protected area.
	Task: Conduct research to discover the possible impact of this new substation on plant life in the protected land. Use electronic media and technology tools to conduct research and gather evidence. Summarize your findings in a report (using a word-processing program) to the electric company's Chief Operating Officer (COO). State whether or not you are in favor of the proposed substation.

ISTE-T (Teachers)

Teachers think of standards as something they need to teach to students. However, in this digital age, students are not the only ones having to learn and know-how to use technology. The ISTE standards for teachers (ISTE-T) define the skills they and other educators must use to teach, work, and learn in an increasingly connected global and digital society. According to the ISTE website (Standards for Teachers 2012), "As technology integration continues to increase in our society, it is paramount that teachers possess the skills and behaviors of digital-age professionals. Moving forward, teachers must become comfortable being co-learners with their students and colleagues around the world."

> The ISTE-T are divided into five categories:
> - Digital Age Citizenship
> - Digital Age Learning
> - Digital Age Work
> - Professional Growth
> - Student Learning

Similar to the ISTE-S standards, each ISTE-T category includes one overarching statement, followed by essential performance indicators for teachers.

The performance indicators are related to the Student Learning category. They are under the heading, "Facilitate and inspire student learning and creativity." They are:

- Promote, support, and model creative and innovative thinking and inventiveness.

- Engage students in exploring real-world issues and solving authentic problems using digital tools and resources.

- Promote student reflection using collaborative tools to reveal and clarify students' conceptual understanding and thinking, planning, and creative processes.

- Model collaborative knowledge construction by engaging in learning with students, colleagues, and others in face-to-face and virtual environments.

The connections between the ISTE-S and ISTE-T standard categories are evident. In order for students to use technology in a creative and innovative manner and apply critical thinking skills, teachers must develop the structure and provide the environment for this type of applied learning to occur. Brief examples of how this might look in the classroom are shown in Figure 2.2. Additionally, subsequent chapters provide substantial supports and examples that teachers can use both to improve their students' learning experiences and to build their own technology-related competencies.

Figure 2.2 Application of Standards for Teachers

Standard	Sample Activity
Standard 1: Creativity and Inventiveness	Use software programs with text, visuals, animation and/or sound applications to create original multimedia vocabulary cards.
Standard 2: Exploring and Solving Real-World Problems	An eleventh grade biotechnology student in San Diego, California used DNA barcoding to help save endangered African wildlife.
Standard 3: Reflection with Collaborative Tools	Take students on an organized nature hike with a digital camera. Working in groups, take pictures of: biotic or abiotic factors, examples of insects or non-insects, cloud formations, and tree leaves. Have students analyze their pictures to create a meaningful summary to share on a class website.
Standard 4: Collaborative Knowledge Construction	Enter class data from a science experiment into one database and graph the class results. Have lab groups analyze and compare their individual, group, and class data.

ISTE-A (Administrators)

Teachers will be glad to know that ISTE outlines essential technology performance indicators not only for them, but also for their immediate supervisors. Ralph Waldo Emerson once said, "What you are speaks so loudly, I can't hear what you are saying." Administrators' actions speak louder than their words. If school leaders expect teachers to learn about, embrace, and use technology as a means to improve student learning, they must demonstrate that they, too, are willing to learn about, embrace, and support teacher use of today's digital tools. According to an online article published by the Department for Education (2013), "Schools with a well-developed vision for learning and which lead and manage their use of technology in support of this are more likely to reap benefits" (para. 4). The role of the school leader is equally as important as that of the classroom teacher if technology integration is to have any lasting positive effects on teaching and learning. To this end, ISTE has outlined several technology standards as they relate to school leadership.

> The categories for these standards are as follows:
>
> - Digital Age Learning
> - Digital Citizenship
> - Professional Practice
> - Systemic Improvement
> - Visionary Leadership

Again, an anchor statement accompanies each category, and this is followed by several related standards.

The following standards are an example of the Visionary Leadership (ISTE, Standards for Administrators) category:

- Inspire and facilitate among all stakeholders a shared vision of purposeful change that maximizes use of digital-age resources to meet and exceed learning goals, support effective instructional practice, and maximize performance of district and school leaders.

- Engage in an ongoing process to develop, implement, and communicate technology-infused strategic plans aligned with a shared vision.

- Advocate on local, state, and national levels for policies, programs, and funding to support implementation of a technology-infused vision and strategic plan.

Implementation of a shared vision can take many forms. Just as teachers use positive reinforcement to encourage students to continue to learn and grow, administrators can acknowledge teachers' efforts to effectively use technology by perhaps including a stellar example in each week's newsletter, creating a school-related blog and posting suggestions examples from teachers around the building, or taking digital photos of students engaged in the creative, effective use of technology to upload onto the school's website. Administrators can encourage, motivate, and inspire teachers to embrace and explore effective use of technology by doing any one or more of the ideas in Figure 2.3. The point is, technology strategies that are good for teachers are also good for administrators.

Figure 2.3 Application of Standards for Administrators

Standard	Sample Activity
Standard 1: Inspire Usage	Acknowledge teachers' efforts by blogging or posting examples and models (which may include photos and/or summaries of student outcomes) in an online newsletter.
Standard 2: Carry Out Strategic Plans	Create a digital collaboration project where teachers and parents can view and post comments to add to the school's technology plan.
Standard 3: Advocate for Technology	Seek out grant opportunities to bring technology into the school; provide technology support through volunteers or school-related personnel; invite guest speakers to work with staff to strengthen and refine effective technology use in the classroom.

Finally, every school building has its go-getters, trendsetters, and trailblazers—teachers who actively seek to try new and innovative resources, techniques, and strategies to support student learning and keep instruction fresh and alive. Administrators can leverage these teacher resources during professional learning communities, lesson studies, team meetings, staff meetings, subject-area (or technology) committee meetings, PTA or school governing committee meetings, or other capacity-building methods to share tried-and-true instructional ideas, strategies, and resources. Teachers-in-the-know can mentor others, share lesson plans or student outcomes, and support their colleagues in any number of ways, usually with minimal time invested. Over time, schools will begin to see a rise in the effective use of technology and, hopefully, in their students' overall achievement.

ISTE-C (Coaches)

While administrators oversee the entire system from teachers to students to staff to parents, coaches are in charge of teachers. ISTE defines coaches as those individuals who support teachers with the integration of technology and help teachers reach the ISTE-T standards.

These categories closely match the instructional supports coaches offer teachers as they directly relate to technology.

The standards for coaches are divided into six categories (ISTE, Standards for Coaches):

- Content Knowledge
- Digital Age Learning
- Digital Citizenship
- Professional Development
- Teaching, Learning, and Assessments
- Visionary Leadership

The Teaching, Learning, and Assessment category calls for coaches to:

- Coach teachers in and model design and implementation of technology-enhanced learning experiences addressing content standards and student technology standards.

- Coach teachers in and model design and implementation of technology-enhanced learning experiences using a variety of research-based, learner-centered instructional strategies and assessment tools to address the diverse needs and interests of all students.

- Coach teachers in and model engagement of students in local and global interdisciplinary units in which technology helps students assume professional roles, research real-world problems, collaborate with others, and produce products that are meaningful and useful to a wide audience.

- Coach teachers in and model design and implementation of technology-enhanced learning experiences emphasizing creativity, higher-order thinking skills and processes, and mental habits of mind (e.g., critical thinking, metacognition, and self-regulation).

- Coach teachers in and model design and implementation of technology-enhanced learning experiences using differentiation, including adjusting content, process, product, and learning environment based upon student readiness levels, learning styles, interests, and personal goals.

- Coach teachers in and model incorporation of research-based best practices in instructional design when planning technology-enhanced learning experiences.

- Coach teachers in and model effective use of technology tools and resources to continuously assess student learning and technology literacy by applying a rich variety of formative and summative assessments aligned with content and student technology standards.

- Coach teachers in and model effective use of technology tools and resources to systematically collect and analyze student achievement data, interpret results, and communicate findings to improve instructional practice and maximize student learning (ISTE 2012, Standards for Coaches).

This set of technology standards assigns coaches the task of coaching and modeling a host of relevant technology uses as they apply to curriculum, instruction, and assessment. For this level of support to occur, coaches must be current in the latest technology trends, have at least some level of competence with technology, and have ideas related to technology integration in all facets of the teaching and learning cycle. Suggested implementation activities follow in Figure 2.4.

A *wiki* is a website that allows for collaborative posts and collaborative editing by those using it.

Figure 2.4 Application of Standards for Coaches

Standard	Sample Activity
Standard 1: Teaching the Standards	Conduct mini-workshops demonstrating where teachers can find interactive lessons online, and how they can save these files for easy access in the future. Better yet, use a wiki and hold discussions online.
Standard 2: Instruction	Model an interactive whiteboard lesson with a class. Work with the teacher to help him or her create another interactive lesson.
Standard 3: Global Outreach	Suggest instructional activities that encourage students to look beyond their own community. For example, when students learn about disaster preparedness, they can research global disasters and analyze relief efforts in various parts of the world.
Standard 4: Critical Thinking	Model how teachers can use online discussion forums to pose thoughtful (and higher-level) reflection questions related to each week's reading assignment, and use the students' posts to drive the classroom discussion.
Standard 5: Differentiation	Demonstrate the use of audio recording software for teachers to use to check students' oral reading fluency.
Standard 6: Instructional Design	Demonstrate for teachers how they can quickly and easily generate note-taking templates and modify them for a variety of classroom uses.
Standard 7: Assessment	Assist a teacher with the development and implementation of an assessment for use with a student response system. Model how to use the response system to provide instant feedback for students.
Standard 8: Student Data	Provide a spreadsheet template with auto-calculations for teachers to enter and easily analyze formative assessment scores.

ISTE-CSE (Computer Science Educators)

According to the ISTE website (2012, Standards for Computer Science Educators), computer science educators are the instructional personnel who ensure that students have a "computing skill set that is applicable across various fields." The following four categories relate to computer science teachers:

- Content Knowledge
- Effective Learning Environments
- Effective Professional Knowledge
- Effective Teaching and Learning

Computer science teachers differ from coaches in that computer science teachers work closely and directly with students. ISTE acknowledges that computer science teachers do not just use technology—they create and design it.

With regard to the Effective Teaching and Learning category, the ISTE-CSE require that computer science educators "demonstrate effective content pedagogical strategies that make the discipline comprehensible to students" (ISTE 2012, Standards for Computer Science Educators).

Seven standards that exemplify effective and engaging practices and methodologies (ISTE 2012, Standards for Computer Science Educators) to plan and teach computer science lessons or units using effective and engaging practices and methodologies are:

- Select a variety of real-world computing problems and project-based methodologies that support active and authentic learning and provide opportunities for creative and innovative thinking and problem solving.

- Demonstrate the use of a variety of collaborative groupings in lesson plans or units and assessments.

- Design activities that require students to effectively describe computing artifacts and communicate results using multiple forms of media.

- Develop lessons and methods that engage and empower learners from diverse cultural and linguistic backgrounds.

- Identify problematic concepts and constructs in computer science and appropriate strategies to address them.

- Design and implement developmentally appropriate learning opportunities supporting the diverse needs of all learners.

- Create and implement multiple forms of assessment and use resulting data to capture student learning, provide remediation, and shape classroom instruction.

So how do these CSE standards compare to the learning standards for teachers? The teaching standards apply to the general use and integration of technology within the curriculum. This means that students in a classroom, whether it be an English or math classroom, should be able to use technology to strengthen their skill set or accomplish some task related to the content in that class. The CSE standards include teaching students how to use technology skills. For example, a social studies teacher cannot expect his or her students to effectively conduct online research if students have not yet been taught how to locate appropriate, relevant, and reliable sites related to the topic. Suggested examples of activities that computer science educators or technology teachers might use with students to develop these essential technology skills are shown in Figure 2.5.

Figure 2.5 Application of Standards for Computer Science Educators

Standard	Sample Activity
Standard 1a: Problem Solving	Have students use 3-dimensional geometry software to apply volume formulas in real-world contexts.
Standard 1b: Collaboration	Have students work with a partner to find and use reliable websites related to a focus topic with specific questions to answer.
Standard 1c: Artifacts	Have students use application software to create a concept map of a topic of study using pictures and text.
Standard 1d: Culture	Have students collect, organize, and summarize data related to the culture and ethnic backgrounds of their town or state.
Standard 1e: Remediation	Having determined that students need extra work with a word processing spell-check program, provide a document with grammar and spelling errors for students to edit.
Standard 1f: Diverse Learning	Assign varied levels of tasks based on students' skill levels. For example, some students might compose a simple word processing document whereas others can begin to use advanced word processing features.
Standard 1g: Assessment	Assign a specific word processing task listing each component that students must complete (i.e., formatting text, formatting document, and inserting visuals). Use the results to plan for further instruction.

Hopefully, schools have CSE teachers or at least have technology personnel support. If so, classroom teachers should touch base with them before assigning technology-related projects to ensure that students have the skill set they need to successfully complete the project. If not, teachers may consider spending some class time instructing students on how to search for and search through Internet resources to find acceptable sites that provide reliable information.

State Technology Standards

Some states have their own set of state technology standards. These standards tend to be in nearly full alignment with the ISTE Standards described previously. In some cases, the standards read exactly the same. In other instances, states have made small revisions, and their standards include slight variations of the ISTE Standards. Figure 2.6 cites one such variation. Other states have a completely unique set of technology standards. Figure 2.7 provides an example of how one standard reads across a primary grade band. Note the intentional scaffolding or step-up design of the skills (e.g., describe, cite examples, describe and give examples) for the concept of "tools for living."

Figure 2.6 Oregon State Technology Standards Compared to the ISTE Standards (Technology Operations and Concepts; 6)

Oregon State Technology Standard	ISTE Standards
Students utilize technology concepts and tools to learn.	Students demonstrate a sound understanding of technology concepts, systems, and operations.

Figure 2.7 Ohio State Technology Standards: The Nature of Technology

Grade	Standard (Technology as Tools)
K	Describe how people use tools to help them do things.
1	Cite examples of how people use tools and processes to perform tasks.
2	Describe and give examples of how people use tools and processes to solve problems.

It is important that teachers know or at least be able to access their state's technology standards. These standards outline the skills students need to successfully navigate through and participate in their digital world.

Common Core State Standards

The ISTE and state technology standards are important because the Common Core State Standards for English Language Arts include statements with regard to technology and digital resources. Students need to have the necessary technology skills outlined in these standards to demonstrate mastery of the Common Core State Standards for English Language Arts that require them to use technology for a specific purpose.

Each grade level has different for English Language Arts standards that directly mention the words *digital*, *multimedia*, and/or *technology*. Teachers whose states have adopted the Common Core State Standards should refer to their grade level's content for specific standards that apply to them. For our purposes, just the anchor standards that include references to technology are listed in Figure 2.8.

Figure 2.8 Technology-Related Common Core State Standards for English Language Arts

Standard	Anchor Standard
Reading Informational Text and Reading Literature	CCSS 7 Integrate and evaluate content presented in diverse formats and *media*, including visually and quantitatively, as well as in words.
Writing	CCSS 6 Use *technology*, including the Internet, to produce and publish writing and to interact and collaborate with others.
Writing	CCSS 8 Gather relevant information from multiple print and *digital* sources, assess the accuracy and credibility of each source, and integrate the information while avoiding plagiarism.
Speaking and Listening	CCSS 5 Make strategic use of *digital* media and visual displays of data to express information and enhance understanding of presentations.

With regard to the Speaking and Listening standards, the Common Core State Standards document notes this:

> New technologies have broadened and expanded the role that speaking and listening play in acquiring and sharing knowledge and have tightened their link to other forms of communication. Digital texts confront students with the potential for continually updated content and dynamically changing combinations of words, graphics, images, hyperlinks, and embedded video and audio. (CCSSO 2010, College and Career Readiness Anchor Standards for Speaking and Listening)

With these thoughts in mind, both technology standards (which require the skills for digital communication) and curriculum standards (which require the application of communication skills) unite to provide a cohesive instructional plan for students of all ages. Likewise, the Common Core State Standards for English Language Arts acknowledge that students are afforded many benefits by learning and communicating through digital means. Therefore, although the technology-related Common Core State Standards for English Language Arts do not appear numerous, they have a strong presence in today's educational arena.

Science, Technology, Engineering, and Mathematics

According to a publication by the International Technology Education Association, ITEA, (2009), an interest in science, technology, engineering, and mathematics (STEM) education initially began with Benjamin Franklin when he wrote that teaching should include subjects such as grafting, planting, commerce, trade, and mechanics. Teachers have been teaching math and science since the early recordings of history. What is less obvious is students' education with regard to technology and engineering. Both subjects are "equal partners within STEM" (ITEA 2009, 2). These subjects, along with science and technology, will "adequately prepare the next generation workforce and produce valued contributors to our communities and society" (2). Technology and engineering provide experiences for students to "apply technology, innovation, design, and engineering in solving societal problems" (2). The engineering process requires students to follow the inquiry process. They must think critically and analytically to solve problems. In doing so, they use technology, and they apply science and math content and skills.

There are no STEM standards, per se. However, this important and relevant topic bears mentioning here as a consideration for teachers wanting to elevate their students' learning experiences, bring meaning to their content knowledge, and integrate technology into the curriculum. Additionally, the infusion of STEM activities in the classroom helps students develop the 21st century skills of collaboration and communication. Note, Chapter 4 offers specific ideas related to STEM and technology integration.

Integrated Technology Lesson Plans

Regardless of whether a teacher is teaching math, science, social studies, or English language arts, the best starting point for developing effective lesson plans is with the standards. These standards define what students should know and be able to do with regard to technology and specific content areas. Teachers generally weave standards into lesson objectives. Ellen Ullman (2011) suggests stating objectives so that students are active participants. For example, in the model lesson plan that follows, teachers might pose this objective to students: "Today, you will conduct online research to discover the engineering principles behind dam construction, and to explore both positive and negative aspects of dams" (How to Plan Effective Lessons).

Following the establishment of the lesson objectives, teachers develop what Ullman refers to as the body of the lesson. This is where teachers devise instructional strategies and activities to lead students to reach the lesson objectives. Ideally, students are active participants in their learning, using lower-level knowledge to attend to higher-level thinking tasks. In the Integrated Technology Lesson Plan Model that follows, students conduct research and apply engineering principles to construct a dam of their own.

The last step to effective instructional planning is what Ullman refers to as reflection. Here, students have time to process what they learned, summarizing key points with classmates and the teacher.

Teachers see how both content and technology standards are connected and how, when students master basic technology skills, these can be integrated easily into a content-area instructional plan. As with all good lesson design, teachers want to "hook" their learners, directly teach students the necessary skills, provide opportunities for exploration and practice, scaffold and support learning as needed, and have an effective evaluation or assessment plan. To illustrate, the following presents an integrated technology lesson plan. An eighth-grade science teacher might use this lesson during a unit on interdependence.

Integrated Technology Lesson Plan Model

Topic: Science and Technology

Standards: CCSS.ELA.W.2, W.4, W.5, W.7, W.8, W.10

Objectives:

- Research and apply the engineering principles behind dam construction.

- Identify how dams positively and adversely affect the environment.

Outcomes:

- Construct a dam using common materials in an attempt to hold water.

- Create a multimedia presentation to explain
  - how engineering contributes to the building of a dam;
  - how dams have positively affected the environment; and
  - how dams have adversely affected the environment.

  Prerequisite Learning Skills: Research, analysis, summarizing, interdependence

Prerequisite Technology Skills: Online research, multimedia presentation, inserting hyperlinks

Materials: Large clear plastic storage container, Internet access, clay, tape, scissors, and other materials the students require to build a model dam

Lesson Steps

1. Review the purpose of and define the term *dam*. Show pictures of both naturally occurring dams and those made by people. Have students predict the effects either has on the environment.

2. Provide resources for students to research the engineering design behind the building of dams. Explain that they should use these engineering principles to construct a model of their own dam. It should hold water on only one side. After their research, students should generate a list of materials that they plan to use to construct their dam. These should be common materials the teacher may provide at school or that students may easily bring from home.

3. Students should also research positive and negative consequences to building dams. They should be able to answer the following questions: Why do people build dams? Who benefits from the construction of dams? Who or what can be harmed by the construction of dams? Do the benefits of dams outweigh the adverse consequences? (Students should justify their ideas.)

4. Have students construct and test their dams.

5. Have students synthesize their learning in a multimedia presentation. This presentation should explain the engineering principles they applied to construct their dam, include a summary of positive and negative consequences of dams, and include hyperlinks to documents, websites, or other resources to support their learning.

6. Evaluate students' success applying engineering principles to construct their dam and their multimedia presentation for completeness and accuracy.

This lesson plan example shows how technology and science (STEM) standards can connect to provide a meaningful and worthwhile learning experience for students. Teachers just beginning to integrate technology into their curriculum should consider starting small and expanding over time. Classroom teachers will also need opportunities to talk with technology teachers to see what skills students have been learning so they can incorporate these skills into the lesson plan.

In the end, teachers should remember that technology integration should enhance students' learning opportunities and simplify their own work.

Conclusion

Instructional standards are a necessary part of the education system. They provide clear goals and objectives so that teachers may develop lessons to provide focused, direct instruction when needed and allow students to be creative with their learning as they communicate ideas digitally. Teachers should know which standards their school or district uses. They should also realize that the CCSS include few but far-reaching technology-related standards as students "go deeper" into the curriculum. By following an effective lesson outline, teachers may be sure they provide the necessary instruction, support, and expectations for students to succeed in today's technology-rich society.

Reflect and Respond

1. Get to know your state's (or the national) technology standards. Find them and read through them. What are your thoughts with regard to these standards?

2. How do you see these standards being addressed in your classroom?

3. What do you believe will be the simplest (and most complicated) technology to integrate into your curriculum? Why?

4. Set a goal for yourself. What do you want to know and be able to do with regard to technology integration? When will you be able to do it?

Chapter 3

Technology to Support Literacy Instruction in English Language Arts

The staff at Edutopia (2007) asked teachers and students, "What technology do you use outside of school that would be good for the classroom? Why? How would that work?" (Join the Conversation). Edutopia lists specific technologies mentioned by respondents. Some may seem to have logical uses in schools, and they may be readily utilized. Others, however, may not seem so obvious, and teachers may not have thought about using these tools in their classrooms. The technologies teachers and students mentioned include:

- Bluetooth
- cell phones
- digital cameras
- flash drives
- graphing calculators
- MP3 players

- laptop computers
- gaming consoles
- public-address systems
- universal remotes
- video cameras
- webcams

This is only a partial list of the technology resources teachers may use with students, and not all teachers may have access to all of these tools. As a result, the focus here will be on ways to integrate technology. The intent is for the options, ideas, and suggestions presented to inspire teachers to move beyond basic applications, such as research reports and drill exercises, and into more creative, thought-provoking activities that will motivate students and engage them with the curriculum at a higher level. Within each content area are ideas to address a myriad of technology standards in an integrated fashion using a host of technology tools. The ideas presented here are intended to inspire teachers to find out more about a particular technology. They could even trigger a related idea using the technology available to them and their students.

> Integrating technology into the curriculum requires thought and attention to several factors, including but not limited to the type of hardware and software available, the amount of hardware (e.g., computers, tablets) available, the availability and use of the hardware, the teacher's grade level, and the level of familiarity of students with the technology. Teachers will need to consider their personal classroom situations and make adjustments to integration techniques and strategies as appropriate.

Technology Integration in Reading

Reading is arguably the most important subject students encounter in school. Even the U.S. Department of Education (2008) urges parents to read at home, stating, "Helping your child become a reader is the single most important thing that you can do to help the child to succeed in school—and in life" (Parents: My Child's Academic Success). When a child can read, he or she can pretty much learn anything that might be of interest. Perhaps a student wants to read a popular series of books, a collection of books by a favorite author, or about a specific topic, such as machines, animals, the solar system, or dinosaurs. Perhaps they even want to keep up with current local events, particularly those that have to do with the local area ecosystem. Reading allows children to be independent learners and thinkers. They can select a book off the shelf, read it, and have a greater sense of knowledge and understanding than they did before.

Reading is also arguably one of the most complex skills to teach. Young students must master elements of phonemic awareness and phonics, which lead to greater reading fluency. Readers must also have a set of strategies to understand unknown words and otherwise make sense of the text as they encounter it. Timothy Shanahan, Douglas Fisher and Nancy Frey (2012) cite vocabulary, sentence structure, coherence (how words and ideas are interconnected), organization, and background knowledge (or lack thereof) as the leading factors that inhibit students from comprehending what they read. All of these factors contribute to what Stephanie Harvey and Anne Goudvis (2007) consider to be the most important aspect of reading: comprehension. As teachers tackle each of these reading elements, they must stay focused on the overall goal of comprehension. One of the notable benefits of incorporating technology into reading instruction is that students can often access a wider variety of reading materials on the Internet than is available in their classroom. As teachers integrate technology into their reading curriculum, the goal does not change. The pitfall for teachers given all of the interactive activities and features that technology-based reading has to offer is that the technology could detract from, rather than strengthen the reading instruction. The following suggestions offer ways for teachers to enhance their reading instruction through the integration of technology. The goal of their lessons drives the choices they make and the use of technology is a supportive tool to further improve students' abilities to read.

Phonemic Awareness, Phonics, and Fluency

Early literacy skills include phonemic awareness (the ability to notice individual sounds) and phonics (the connection between written and spoken language) (ReadingRockets. org). As students learn to decode words that follow specific patterns, they improve their fluency rates, and they are able to apply decoding strategies to words that do not follow a standard pattern or words that break the pattern. Many of these early reading skills focus on application. Therefore, much of the technology available to support teachers with this level of reading instruction is game-like or interactive practice, representative of drill exercises. Even so, teachers can use technology to encourage development of 21st century learning skills.

> *Phonemic awareness* is the ability to notice individual sounds. *Phonics* is the connection between written and spoken language (ReadingRockets.org).

The following examples show teachers how to utilize technology resources to develop, reinforce, and/or extend phonemic awareness, phonics, and fluency skills in their students.

- Students can use websites to practice phoneme manipulation (the smallest unit of speech) and build letter–sound recognition.

- Students can access read–aloud books and websites that provide auditory support to build decoding and word–recognition skills.

- Some read–aloud sites provide drill–like practice games, such as matching, for students to read beginning words.

- Some sites require students to think about what they are reading and prove their comprehension of the text.

- Other sites offer story creation where students fill in the blanks, creating a unique story comprised of their chosen words.

- Some sites offer stories in other languages.

- Some sites offer printable activity pages.

- Online stories may include animations, interactive page turning, audio, pop–up vocabulary definitions, and many other interactive features.

- Students can access rhyming websites to practice typing words and then finding words that rhyme. These sites have drop–down menus of words, so students do not need to spell a word perfectly in order to find it. They can begin to type the word, and then find and select the word from the online database. Students can record words that fit a particular word family and/or record words that have similar sounds but do not fit the word family. Figure 3.1 shows a three–column graphic organizer used to sort words that rhyme with *wait*. Students must use critical thinking skills to identify three different spellings of words and then categorize them according to spellings.

Figure 3.1 Recording Rhyming Words and Sorting by Word Families

–ait	–ate	–eight
wait	crate	freight
gait	gate	weight
trait	slate	

These reading websites also provide multi-syllable words practice. Teachers in intermediate grades can use these sites to enhance their instruction with regard to this skill. Students can record themselves reading pretty much anything using audio recording software. When the audio is stored on a data storage site or downloaded onto a flash or jump drive, teachers can listen to it at a convenient time instead of taking class time to listen to each student read. If the teacher has a copy of the text in front of him or her, the teacher may complete a formal running record, obtain an accuracy rate and a reading rate, and analyze error patterns.

Vocabulary

Research on vocabulary learning has identified three "tiers" of words (Hutton 2008). Tier 1 words are basic, non-multiple-meaning words. These are words we hear and use in everyday life. Words like *coat*, *kitchen*, and *thunderstorm* are Tier 1 words. Tier 2 words are fairly common words but do not necessarily come up in everyday conversation. These are general terms that students may or may not need direct instruction on in order to comprehend a particular passage, such as *particular*, *bargain*, *creek*, and *tuck*. Tier 2 words also include multiple-meaning words. Students may know what a *plant* is (living thing that grows in the ground), but do they know what a *plant* is (factory). Conversely, Tier 3 words are content-specific words, words that generally arise only during a discussion about a particular topic, such as *estuary*, *evaporation*, and *igneous*. They are used infrequently and may never come up in everyday conversation. Teachers likely spend time teaching Tier 2 and Tier 3 words that are essential for students to know for the complete comprehension of a text or subject. Teachers may use different strategies for direct vocabulary instruction to build students' independent reading skills. The integration of technology can both support and extend students' vocabulary acquisition and give them tools to use when they come upon an unknown or unfamiliar word.

and extend students' vocabulary acquisition and give them tools to use when they come upon an unknown or unfamiliar word.

The following suggestions demonstrate how to integrate technology into vocabulary instruction.

- Rhyming websites can build students' vocabulary skills. One strategy named after Dorothy Frayer from the University of Wisconsin is the Frayer Model (Frederick and Klausmeier 1969). Students include a definition, characteristics, examples, and non-examples in each of four boxes surrounding a word. This model is intended to lead students to a deeper understanding of terms as well as relationships between words in their own lives. Modifications on this model include inserting a picture or using the term in an original sentence. Students can find definitions, synonyms, and antonyms for words from both rhyming sites and online dictionary sites by selecting this option.

Figure 3.2 Example of a Frayer Model Using Words from Online Resources

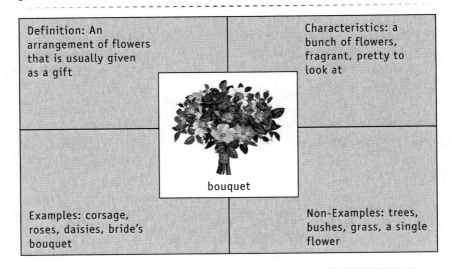

- Word walls are a popular instructional strategy that teachers use to build and reference key words within a content area or throughout a unit of study, especially in the primary grades. However, Janis M. Harmon et al. (2009) advocate for their use with middle level and secondary students as well. In a study of forty-four seventh graders in two sections of heterogeneously grouped reading classes in suburban south-central Texas, students said they used their classroom word wall "for studying, remembering, writing, and completing classroom assignments" (401).

- Students can use online resources and application software, such as word processors or multimedia slides, to develop their own working set of digital vocabulary cards. These can also be printed and posted in the classroom for easy reference. In addition to including a term and its definition, students can find images or other visual representations of the term. Another option is to have students use a digital camera to find examples of terms around their classroom, campus, or home to download and insert as part of their vocabulary study. This element helps students gain ownership of their learning and encourages creative thinking as they attempt to find examples of ideas around them.

- Students can use poster-making software either on the computer (e.g., Kidspiration and Inspiration) or online (Glogster EDU) to develop concept maps that use the terms they need to learn.

- Word clouds, graphical representations of text, allow students to work collaboratively and can be utilized to preview key vocabulary before reading, check for understanding during reading, and demonstrate mastery after reading. (See example in Figure 3.3.)

- WordSift (see example in Figure 3.4) enables students to sift vocabulary into various formats, incorporate images, highlight words, and provide examples within the original text's context.

Figure 3.3 Tricky Words Word Cloud (Created in Wordle)

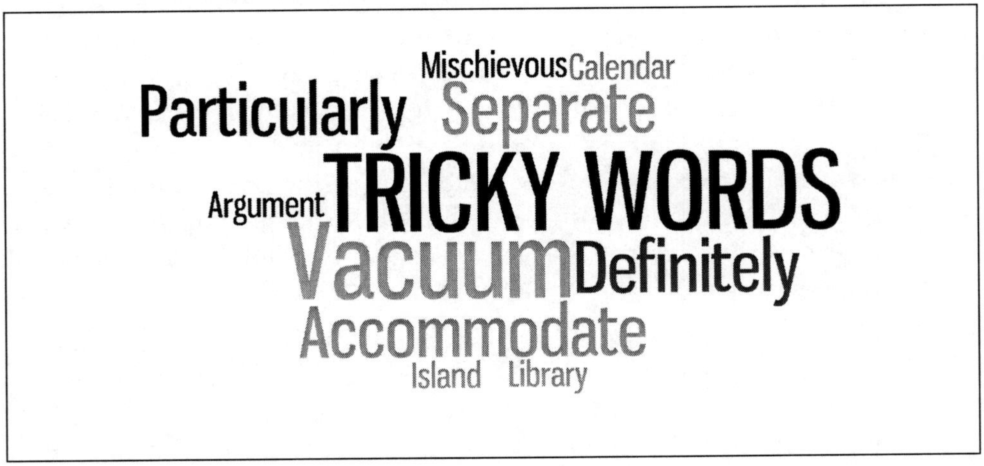

Mischievous Calendar
Particularly Separate
Argument TRICKY WORDS
Vacuum Definitely
Accommodate
Island Library

Figure 3.4 Completed WordSift for "I Have A Dream" Speech by Dr. Martin Luther King, Jr. (www.wordsift.com)

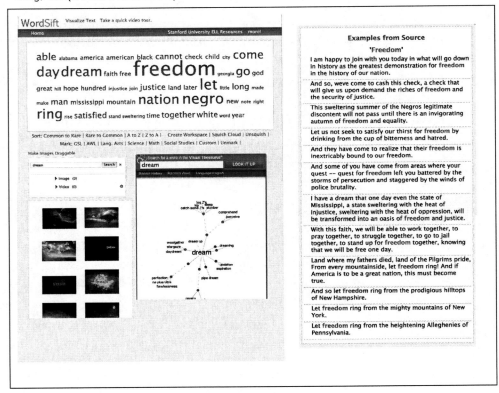

Book Study

According to the University of Texas online library page, "An author study is a unit lesson that gives students the opportunity to delve deeply into an author's life and body of work" ("What is an Author Study?"). This may be completed independently by students, in small groups, or as a class. Teachers can use author studies to help students develop their overall reading skills. By reading multiple texts by the same author, students can analyze and compare characters, illustrations, and themes. Teachers can also differentiate instruction since most authors write books on similar themes or topics at varied reading levels. Many children's book authors and publishers of children's books have their own websites. These sites include information, book reviews, games, activities, blogs, and a variety of other resources. Aside from author sites, some publishers have sites that offer activities and ideas for learning extensions that directly support literacy in the classroom.

Teachers can find websites related to their favorite authors at:

- Authors and Illustrators on the Web, http://www.djusd.k12.ca.us/harper/jboston/AuthorsandIllustratorsontheWeb.htm

- Scholastic's Author and Illustrator Index, http://www.scholastic.com/librarians/ab/biolist.htm

In addition to examining an author's body of work, comparisons between genres of the same title are beneficial to deepen student understanding of a text and tap into higher-order thinking skills. Since many well-known and popular children's books have been made into movies, teachers can have students compare the experiences, facts, events, and development of mood of reading a select text versus watching the movie. Alternatively, teachers can have students read both a book and a movie review, and compare them as far as their abilities to persuade would-be readers and watchers, respectively. Teachers could have students create a visual and/or audio advertisement for a particular story, and then compare it to the trailer for the movie version of the book. Students might even read blogs and contribute to them, addressing Common Core State Standards for English Language Arts Writing Standard 6 to "use technology, including the Internet, to produce and publish writing and to interact and collaborate with others" (CCSSO 2010).

General Reading Support

Of course, the overall goal of any reading instruction is to have students read and understand a variety of genres. Phonemic awareness, phonics, fluency, and vocabulary skills all synchronize to support comprehension. Technology can do more to support general reading skills besides simply reading texts. The Common Core State Standards for English Language Arts in Reading Standard 7 require students to "integrate and evaluate content presented in diverse media and formats, including visually and quantitatively, as well as in words" (CCSSO 2010). Technology is the perfect tool to accomplish this task.

The following suggestions offer useful reading support.

- While students can certainly type responses to questions or summarize stories using word-processing software, there are even more tools available to add depth and complexity to technology usage. For example, with VoiceThread, students can post responses to an online bulletin board or classroom website. Here, viewers post collaborative, interactive slide shows that include images, documents, and sound files. Viewers from around the world can comment on others' work or create a project of their own which others may comment.

- To meet the needs of students embarking on an unfamiliar experience (e.g., Texas students learning about the Canadian wilderness), the Internet is the perfect place to begin building that necessary background knowledge. Students can read short informational articles, view photos and videos, and even listen to an interview before beginning a new book that involves unfamiliar subject matter. Students can also research specific information related to a story or nonfiction text and create a short presentation for the class.

- Electronic books, or eBooks, bring a new dimension to reading. Students find eBooks appealing and, thus, are more eager to read and spend time reading (Fasimpaur 2003). Additionally, Kathleen Roskos et al. (2014, discussion, para. 2) cite research indicating that recent studies of young children using eBooks "show the benefits of audiovisual synchrony in supporting attention to eBook content to achieve early literacy outcomes." This is likely because eBooks have special features which make them interactive. These include built-in dictionaries, read-aloud tools, bookmarks, note-taking tools, hyperlinks, and the ability to digitally search. Students can adjust the size of the text, while the devices used to view eBooks can store numerous volumes. Additionally, students can read an assigned text and respond to questions the teacher has embedded in the text. The use of eBooks in the classroom, in theory, will lead to increased reading, which in turn will lead to improvements in students' overall reading skills.

- As new standards are developed and used both nationally and by individual states, the requirement to use a balance between literature and informational text is expected. Oftentimes, teachers try to connect fiction and nonfiction by topic or theme. Online resources can provide informational passages of text related to a fictional story. For example, students reading *Charlotte's Web* by E. B. White can read informational text about the barn spider. Students reading *Charlie and the Chocolate Factory* by Roald Dahl can read about how chocolate and other confections are made, and then create a how-to summary of the process.

- Educational publishers have devised digital learning programs specifically for reading. They can run online or through a school or district server. Generally, students begin by taking an initial assessment. The program places students at their respective suitable starting point. Then students complete a series of digital lessons and activities, reassessing along the way. The program responds to students as needed, increasing or decreasing in difficulty, or providing additional practice with a specific skill. These digital learning systems are not intended to replace direct classroom instruction; rather, they work alongside the teacher and support students in their needed skill areas.

- Much of today's literature has been made into movies. After reading a book that has an accompanying movie, students can use the movie trailer to synthesize main events, summarize the story, or compare their view of the story with the movie producer's view. Movie trailers offer a short synopsis of the contents of the movie. Students can explain in writing how the events presented in the trailer compare to the events they would have included, had they created the trailer. They can also evaluate the trailer with regard to how well it "sells" the movie. Does it make the movie seem more or less interesting than the book? Would you recommend reading the book or watching the movie? Why?

It would be remiss not to address the challenges teachers face in incorporating technology use to enhance student learning, particularly in schools with only a few student computer stations and/or limited lab space. Finding time during the school day for students to access these programs can certainly present a barrier to implementing technology, especially on a regular basis. Some possible options include scheduling predictable, routine lab times specifically for this purpose, or even opening the lab before and after school to provide additional opportunities.

Poetry

April is National Poetry Month. This is a delightful reason for teachers to infuse some poetry reading and writing into the curriculum. As early as kindergarten, students should be able to recognize text as a poem (Common Core State Reading Standards Literature Anchor 5). Many poets have their own websites, which teachers may use to introduce poetry or to support student learning of poetry. Some authors include written poetry as well as podcasts (audio readings) of poems on their sites. This is a useful tool for special needs students, English language learners, or struggling readers who may benefit from hearing poetry in addition to reading it. Poetry sites also may include interactive features such as poetry building and language skill games to make poetry reading more entertaining while students read, write, and apply various reading and language arts skills.

The following are some examples of poetry websites.

- **Kenn Nesbitt's Poetry for Kids (Grades K–5):** On his website, Kenn Nesbitt has links to poems he has written, which readers may sort by category; poetry (word and language) games; summaries of interviews he has had with other authors; poetry apps; news (recent posts of his); podcasts (audio recordings of poems); activities, lessons, and quizzes; a dictionary of poetry terms as well as a rhyming dictionary; survey results of poetry-related surveys; and videos. He has contests for members, articles for parents and teachers, and information regarding school visits. Classrooms too far away to schedule an in-person visit may request a Skype visit.

- **Emily Dickinson Museum (Grades 6–12):** The Emily Dickinson Museum website offers students who visit a poem-of-the-week word search, access to information about Ms. Dickinson's life, and tips on reading her work. Readers may find historical facts about when and where Dickinson lived, search for poems by topic, and even read about current events related to Dickinson's work. (Did you know, actor Bill Murray read Dickinson poetry to a group of construction workers in May 2009?)

- **Poetry Foundation (Grades K–12):** Students who visit the Poetry Foundation website may discover information about the life of any poet they are studying, as well as read or access podcasts and videos of selected poems of famous (and lesser known) poets. The site even has a link devoted especially to children's poetry.

According to Carol Clark (2010), poetry offers both a "psychological and intellectual reward" for readers (1). Students who read poetry have an opportunity to explore language beyond the more structured formats of stories and essays. This is because of the varied (and sometimes unusual) diction, syntax, and text used by poets. Clark states, "Older students benefit from the language study and attention to detail that both the poems and the students' responses demand" (1). Students can access poetry information and games online. The interactivity of some websites can act to inspire students, provide visual interest, and engage them more fully in poetry than simply reading it in a book.

The following are some suggestions for integrating poetry and technology.

- After listening to a podcast of a poem, students can choose a poem for themselves, practice, rehearse, and record it as a digital file using audio recording software. Teachers with classroom websites can post the students' recordings to their webpage.

- Students can assemble a digital database of poetry websites that they can suggest to other classes in the school.

- After listening to a particular poem, students can search for music files online that reflect the mood of the poem. For example, if a poem is funny or makes them feel happy, students might find an upbeat tune or song to represent it. If a poem is more melancholy or serious, students can find a slower, sadder-sounding tune or song for it. Then students can recite their poem to the class (or record it) with music playing softly in the background.

- Students can research and find three or more poems by three different authors online that are related by theme. Students can reference these poems or make digital copies of them, if permitted, and compare the topics and how each author uses language to develop the poem. If they are typing in a word-processing program, students may use a note-taking function to identify specific areas of the poem they choose to discuss in their summary.

- Student pairs can collaborate to make a video presentation of a poem. One student records himself or herself introducing a particular poem. In the introduction, the student should include the name of the poem, the author, and a brief description of the contents of the poem. Then a second student can recite the poem. These videos may be aired on a school television show or viewed by another class.

Differentiated Reading Instruction

Guided reading is a successful differentiating strategy (Pinnell and Fountas 2008). Technology has a role here as well as with whole-group instruction. According to David Rose (2004), technology can provide the individual support and guidance students need to be successful with the reading material assigned to them. "New reading technologies can extend the reach of the teacher, ensuring that every student is engaged, highly engaged, in meaningful independent practice that optimizes their development as confident, skillful, and motivated readers" (2). He identifies four factors of reading support that "apprentice" readers need to be successful:

1. Models of skilled reading and writing

2. Meaningful practice in reading and writing

3. Scaffolds that support learning and that can gradually be released as skills develop

4. Timely and appropriate feedback on performance

The following strategies offer teachers options for integrating technology into their differentiated classrooms.

- Digital reading packaged programs are useful. These technology-based reading programs provide instructional supports unique to each individual student.

- Online resources provide an alternative to expensive individualized reading and language arts packaged programs. Programs such as Raz-Kids from Reading A-Z are web-based and provide reading support for students at their instructional levels. They offer single classroom accounts at lower rates than larger packaged programs that might offer only school or district accounts.

- Tablets or eReaders can be used as an independent learning follow-up activity or as center-type activities to support and extend learning by inviting students to annotate their text or record themselves reading a portion of it for fluency practice.

- Students can use the interactive reading features, take notes, mark text, or apply any other suitable interactive reading task that supports their comprehension. As an independent learning follow-up, students may re-access stories and text to answer a set of comprehension questions, write in response to text, or take an online quiz. Students can complete digital graphic organizers or run through digital vocabulary flash cards as part of their independent work.

- During centers or center-type activities, students can complete a puzzle or play an online learning game related to the reading skills they are practicing that day or that week. Students might also take part in an online discussion forum, as in a digital literature circle where students connect electronically through writing or texting using an instant messaging program.

- Students can access teacher-assigned online reading games and activities for additional practice.

- Teachers can save differentiated graphic organizers in a file for themselves to use with different groups of students. Similarly, students can download the appropriate graphic organizer on their own digital device to complete individually.

Technology Integration in Language Arts and Writing

Students in this digital age need to learn how to write using software programs (Common Core State Standards Writing Standard 6). As connected as some teachers may be to paper-and-pencil tasks, they need to understand that technology may soon be the norm in classrooms across the United States. In a survey of nearly 2,500 Advanced Placement (AP) and National Writing Project (NWP) teachers, Kristen Purcell, Judy Buchanan, and Linda Friedrich (2013) report that digital tools are positively impacting what and how students write. The teachers they surveyed acknowledge that students have a greater investment in what they write, and greater engagement in the writing process when they use technology. In fact, today's teenagers write constantly, especially if one considers email, social media posts, and text messaging *writing*. According to Amanda Lenhart et al. (2008), "Most teenagers spend a considerable amount of their life composing texts, but they do not think that a lot of the material they create electronically is *real* writing" (para. 4). At the same time, these same teens believe that writing is an essential skill for one to achieve success in life.

Teachers know that their students use technology to write and write often. Likewise, the use of technology is a required national standard, and students value the opportunities they know good writing will bring them in their futures. Therefore, teachers should have some language arts and writing technology ideas in their teacher toolbox to start moving on a digital path. Some suggestions for integrating technology into reading have led teachers to have students write in response to reading. This section explores options for integrating technology as a means for students to compose larger projects, such as reports, essays, and comprehensive projects.

The following examples show how teachers can use technology to build and support language skills such as grammar, spelling, punctuation, and word study.

- Teachers can set up an interactive blog site where they pose a question for students to answer or make a statement about a topic. In turn, students post their responses, advice, or suggestions. For example, a teacher may write a blog related to his or her homework policies. Then he or she may make a statement about the importance of completing homework followed by a question: "Sometimes it's hard to get motivated to do homework. What tips do you have to get geared up to complete your homework?" (Ironically, answering this question would actually be the students' homework for the night.)

This strategy also supports literacy instruction when the teacher posts a comment or question for students to consider with regard to a narrative or informational text the students are reading. An independent follow-up activity might require students to post a blog response. Once logged in, students can read their classmates' posts and respond.

- Online global learning communities allow students to access a Writing Center and choose from an assortment of tasks, including writing a movie review or introducing others to their hometown. Students can read others' posts or articles, connect with poets and authors, play interactive writing and language arts–related games, take quizzes, watch author videos, and join discussion groups. Regardless of the activity they are taking part in, students write to share their work or converse with or respond to other writers.

- Instead of putting together a slide show or completing a text-based project using a word-processing or desktop-publishing program, students can write, edit, create, and publish their own eBook using a website.

- When teachers and students are stuck for creative writing ideas, need support for writers' notebook lessons, or want to access a new mentor text, they can turn to websites specifically devoted to this level of support. Such sites provide lessons, resources, and prompt starters. Teachers and students can find information related to the writing process, writing traits, and different genres of writing.

- Teachers can help students practice their spelling lists by using sites specifically designed for this. Once a spelling list is added, students can play learning activities and games as well as take tests online. As an instructional support, this requires just a few moments of the teacher's time, and students can access it from school or home.

- Students can access online games that support grammar and mechanics skills.

Information Literacy

Information literacy refers to students' abilities to know when there is a need for information. They must be able to identify, locate, evaluate, and effectively use the information they find as it relates to an issue or problem (Weis 2003). The American Library Association (2013) advocates for a parallel curriculum specific to information literacy skills. This curriculum ensures that students know when they need information and when they do not; how to access appropriate information efficiently and effectively, and be able to exclude nonessential ideas; use technological skills as a means to an end; analyze and evaluate information for accuracy and usefulness, thus becoming more confident, proficient masters of information gathering. Students can become overwhelmed in what David Schenk (1997) coined *data smog*, where too much information keeps us stopped in our tracks, and we are unable to see where we are going. Therefore, as students learn through digital means, teachers (e.g., classroom teachers, media specialists, technology specialists) should instruct them in the process of gathering information so they learn the skills to find information they need relevant to their task.

The University of Idaho (2014) has compiled a series of modules intended to teach information literacy to anyone interested in learning more about this skill set. The skills taught are outlined clearly in each module's objectives and summarize the content of information literacy instruction. An edited, simplified version is found in Figure 3.5.

Figure 3.5 The Purpose and Relevance of Information Literacy

Purpose	
• understand the difference between scholarly and popular information	• know how to cite sources on the path to finding information
• distinguish between primary and secondary sources	• know how to evaluate information (and its authors) for its accuracy, authenticity, relevance
• know how information is formatted	
• know how and when to broaden or narrow a topic	• keep track of sources
• use key words to help find information	• be able to avoid plagiarism
• know and understand the uses of databases	• be able to acquire resources from libraries and other digital storehouses

As teachers, we ask students to research information all the time. But how often do we model and instruct students on how to effectively conduct this research? The world of information is wide and vast. It is easy to understand how students may get lost, misguided, or displaced as they attempt to access the information they need. Direct instructional techniques, modeling, and guided and independent practice should be part of students' overall learning experience when they are asked to conduct research or otherwise access specific information online. Information literacy skills do not stand alone. We teach the skills so that students can navigate the information (text) on their path to becoming independent thinkers (and readers).

Conclusion

Learning to read and write, and continuing to develop literacy skills are the mainstays of students' education from kindergarten through twelfth grade. While technology can support and extend students' thinking, teachers should not lose sight of the goal of literacy instruction to improve reading and writing skills so that students can become independent readers and thinkers. In addition, information literacy plays a critical role in students' productive, effective, and efficient use of technology. Teachers should provide direct instruction and adequate learning opportunities for students to become productive, efficient, and effective users of online resources to gather information for a specific purpose. The technology is available for teachers to use with students—all they need to do is step forward and engage students with meaningful technology-driven work.

Reflect and Respond

1. In the past, how have you used technology to support reading and language arts instruction?

2. What new or improved integrated technology ideas can you use to support reading and language arts instruction?

3. When thinking about how you responded to question 2, what learning goal or objective will this technology support?

4. If a teacher does not know how to integrate technology into his or her literacy block, what suggestions would you give this teacher to get started? Why? What learning goals or objectives does this suggestion support?

Chapter 4

Technology to Support Content-Area Instruction

Technology integration does not only apply to reading, writing, and media literacy skills, it also applies to content-area instruction. Most of what we use technology for is to communicate (read, write, listen, and sometimes speak). Technology has a natural pairing with literacy. If we think about the content areas in terms of communicating information (reading and writing), then technology has many more valuable uses besides skill-and-drill games. This chapter explores how technology is as valuable a learning tool in the content areas as it is in literacy and how it deserves equal time and attention to help students learn, grow, and think.

Content-area teachers should be aware of the value online games bring to learning. They help students practice, learn, and extend their knowledge. According to a study by the MacArthur Foundation (2011), 51 percent of students said gaming technologies made it easier for them to understand difficult concepts. Likewise, collaboration is a necessary 21st century skill. This same study found that about one-third of teenagers who used the Internet have, at one time or another, shared the content they produced. With the increased popularity of social networking applications and websites, this number is likely growing.

Technology Integration in Mathematics

As referenced in Chapter 3, many computer software programs can personalize reading practice for students. Teachers may also be familiar with skill-building websites and software that support the acquisition of basic facts and the application of general math skills. There are some tried-and-true favorites among educators and their students, and new products come on the market constantly. Some work on servers and some are web-based. Some are mostly skill-driven, while others offer students tutorials and opportunities to earn rewards as they "pass" on to the next level.

These types of programs are customary in schools across the United States. The National Mathematics Advisory Panel was created in 2006 by President Bush to advise the president and the secretary of education on the best use of scientifically-based research to advance the teaching and learning of mathematics. The panel's 2008 report, "Foundations for Success: The Final Report of National Mathematics Advisory Panel," outlines several key aspects of mathematical teaching and learning related to curriculum, student learning, teacher education, instructional practices and materials, assessment, and policies. This report points out that technologically driven tutorials are successful when they are designed to help specific populations of students meet specific goals. For this reason, the report warns teachers to be mindful that the software they use be proven successful with the students with whom they intend to use it.

Technology Integration to Support Math Concepts and Skills

Computers cannot replace the caring nature of the classroom teacher. They can, however, support the teacher as he or she provides direct instruction in mathematical processes and applications. The Internet is filled with lessons, activities, online learning games, how-to videos, and tutorials related to any and all math topics. A teacher's current math textbook likely has accompanying online resources. These tend to be program specific and limited with regard to the quantity of instructional support. Online, teachers and students can find just the right instruction, tutorial, or practice activities (printable pages or online interactive activities) to solidify and extend mathematical concepts learned in the classroom. Online, teachers and students can find just the right instruction (interactive demonstrations, videos, and audios), tutorials (walk-throughs), or practice activities (printable pages or online interactive activities) with immediate feedback to solidify and extend mathematical concepts learned in the classroom. Khan Academy is one such popular resource. On YouTube, these mini-lessons walk students step-by-step through many advanced mathematical processes.

Teachers can use interactive online games to have students gain confidence and mastery of a particular skill. Allie Bidwell, writer for *U.S. News and World Report*, interviewed Jessica Lindl, general manager of the digital gaming company GlassLab and a spokesperson for the game SimCityEDU. In Bidwell's article (2013), Jessica Lindl identifies one key reason gaming is so popular with teachers, students, and parents to supplement instruction: regular, immediate, and positive feedback. For example, students may have to match the sum with the proper addends or factors with products. When they do, they may be rewarded with an entertaining animation. This also allows for differentiation. Choosing a level within a game or program can individualize many math games and maximize student learning. If teachers have access to independent student computer workstations, handheld devices, or interactive whiteboards (IWBs), students can "play" and have fun while reinforcing essential skills, both in the classroom and at home. The teacher can monitor students' activities, and students can receive immediate corrective feedback. The web is filled with math games for all skill levels and on all topics.

Favorite Online Math Games

- Cool Math Games: http://www.coolmath-games.com
- Funbrain Math Arcade: http://www.funbrain.com/brain/MathBrain/MathBrain.html
- Funbrain Math Baseball: http://www.funbrain.com/math/index.html
- IXL: http://www.ixl.com
- Math Play: http://www.math-play.com
- Math Playground: http://www.mathplayground.com

Online games provide an interactive element to learning math. Additionally, teachers can use online manipulatives to teach math concepts. These may be displayed and manipulated with the class, or, with the use of an interactive whiteboard or hand-held device, students may personally utilize the materials in an interactive manner. For example, base-ten blocks provide tactile, concrete, hands-on manipulation of numbers. Students can "make trades," physically move them across place values on the screen, and watch math happen in front of them. When students start interacting with numbers bigger than 1,000, tangible blocks become cumbersome and quantitatively unmanageable. Fortunately, online resources take care of this problem.

Teachers can use virtual manipulatives to teach students pretty much anything and everything they need to know about math that can possibly be demonstrated through concrete examples. Although students do not get to touch and physically manipulate the numbers or figures, they can still "see" math happening in front of them and manipulate the tools through virtual means. One popular math manipulative website is the National Library of Virtual Manipulatives (NLVM). This site has manipulatives divided by grade bands (preK–2, 3–5, 6–8, and 9–12) and domains (number and operations, algebra, geometry, measurement, and data analysis and probability). Teachers can access base-ten blocks, number chips (for both positive and negative integers), fraction bars, number lines, and grids. Whatever manipulatives a teacher may need, he or she can find it at the NLVM site.

Online Support for Differentiating Math Instruction

With great exception to a class's makeup, no one math lesson can possibly meet the needs of all students. Differentiation refers to teachers providing instructional support for students' varied learning needs. We repeat and reteach skills and concepts to those who do not grasp them; we enrich and extend thinking and learning for those who excel.

Carol Ann Tomlinson (2005), in an article for the National Middle School Association, defines differentiation as having clear learning goals for all students "that are rich in meaning and provide various avenues and support systems to maximize the chance of each student succeeding with those rich and important goals" (14).

Technology can greatly enhance learning experiences for students who arrive to math class with varied math skills. Software programs, online games, and practices that target specific skill needs provide the support and enrichment to help math teachers help their students reach their goals.

We have to teach whatever we teach so that kids who struggle with it emerge with its important understandings and skills in their grasp. We also have to teach whatever we teach so that students who grasp it with uncanny speed can experience and surmount personal challenge. (Tomlinson 2005, 13)

While purchased software programs can provide individualized math instruction, remediation, practice, and extended learning opportunities for students, web-based resources offer the same. Teachers can find, bookmark, and assign the sites for targeted individualized use within the classroom and as at-home practice. They can also use these in a small-group instruction setting. Here, students learn, review, and practice collaboratively to solve problems with direct or indirect teacher monitoring.

For paper-based support, teachers can access online resources to find applicable practice pages that can be easily downloaded, often for free. For example, some students may need additional practice with 2- and 3-digit numbers, while others are ready for 4- and 5-digit numbers and a few need work with 6-digit numbers. The teacher may easily print practice pages to meet the specific learning needs (and goals) for these students. Lower elementary students working on regrouping may vary in their needs as well. Some students may need double-digit practice, while others are ready for triple-double and triple-triple problems. Lower elementary students working above grade level in basic addition and subtraction can be given work with more advanced problems, or they may begin working on multiplication and division concepts. Because the Internet provides access to so many practice and skill pages, teachers can differentiate math practice easily. Many of these resources come in Portable Document Format (PDF) or as common word-processing documents, so teachers can save them to a folder, title them clearly, and have them ready for subsequent school years, streamlining their advanced preparation time.

Graphing Programs

Teachers and students can use various graphing programs to graph data. For example, spreadsheet programs are well suited for graphing data and are convenient since they come standard on most operating systems. Young students can use them to record small amounts of data; older students can use them to record, organize, manipulate, calculate, and chart data. Young students can use a drawing program such as KidPix or Microsoft Paint to create simple pictographs or bar graphs using line tools and stamps (images) to show how many times they roll a die or how many students prefer vanilla, chocolate, or strawberry ice cream. Older students can enter daily high and low temperatures in a spreadsheet program and create a double line graph of the data, formatting the lows with a blue line and the highs with a red line. Students who need to organize and calculate large amounts of data can enter a calculation formula following the program's built-in wizards. Then, when new data is entered, the calculation fields simply continue to include the additional data. No extra work necessary. Students can choose the data they want to include in a chart and decide upon the best chart option and chart features to display their data.

Teachers can use online graphing programs, such as "Create a Graph" from the National Center for Education Statistics or graphing software programs such as "The Graph Club" by Tom Snyder Productions, to teach graphing through technology.

Figure 4.1 shows how students can use Microsoft Excel to calculate the value over time of an initial investment of $1,000 at 5 percent, 8 percent, and 10 percent interest. Once the investing calculations are made, students can compare the data. (Notice how doubling the interest rate does not double the investment after ten years.)

Figure 4.1 Using Excel to Calculate Compound Interest

	A	B	C
1	5%	8%	10%
2	1000	1000	1000
3	1050	1080	1100
4	1102.5	1166.4	1210
5	1157.625	1259.712	1331
6	1215.506	1360.489	1464.1
7	1276.282	1469.328	1610.51
8	1340.096	1586.874	1771.561
9	1407.1	1713.824	1948.717
10	1477.455	1850.93	2143.589
11	1551.328	1999.005	2357.948

In addition to spreadsheet software, schools may have access to server-based, stand-alone, or online tools. Software and online graphing programs may include simple, step-by-step directions, making their functionality more realistic. Teachers and students can find and use exactly the graphing format they need to display their data. For example, a more advanced online graphing program places comparable data into a scatter plot. Not only can students easily see the regression toward the mean with the click of a button, but they can also discover the algebraic equation related to that line. Then, students can use the computer-generated formula to predict with X percent of certainty how the data calculates when they know one variable. One online graphing program is GeoGebra. It is free and appropriate for students from elementary through college levels. It includes applications for geometry, algebra, statistics, and calculus.

One last piece of mathematical-based technology worth mentioning is the stand-alone graphing calculator. While these devices have been around for many years, over time they have evolved into versatile tools that students can use for a variety of functions, including graphing complex formulas, such as conic graphing, solving equations, and operating business functions. Additionally, with an attachment, such as a calculator-based ranger (CBR), students can attach this device to their graphing calculator to gather sound-wave data to write sine and cosine functions. Math is not the only content area supported by technology. Science instruction, often closely linked with math, is enhanced with technology.

Technology Integration in Science

The National Science Teachers Association (NSTA 2010) advocates for science and technology instruction in schools, specifically within the context of personal and societal issues. They state, "Science and technology are central to our well-being and success as individuals, as members of society, and as members of the global community" (1). They suggest, among other scientific and technologically relevant means, to "incorporate the practices and understanding of scientific inquiry and technological design" (3). In this author's opinion, science and technology are inextricably linked; one cannot "do science" without the technology and tools available to answer scientific questions. Advances in technology, such as digital microscopes and digital scales, serve to enhance students' observations of the world around them and provide for more precise measurements as they collect and analyze data.

Science learning can depend on mathematical applications. For example, students may learn about evaporation by watching, observing, and reading. Students might record an initial amount of water in different-sized containers and measure the water again after twenty-four, forty-eight, and seventy-two hours. Here, students need to record data and track it, likely through some sort of graph. They do so because the information they have gathered will be used to support or refute a hypothesis. Students might maintain data on animal populations, rainfall amounts, temperatures, or any other topic as it relates to a particular scientific inquiry. Therefore, any of the graphing integrations mentioned earlier apply in science instruction as well.

In addition to graphing tools, teachers can find and use instructional lessons and activities online to support science learning. Some sites, such as BrainPOP, BrainPOP Jr., and Gizmos, require a subscription. Other sites, such as NOVA and PBS LearningMedia (formerly PBS Teachers' Domain), are free. Such websites can offer instructional lessons, video demonstrations, interactive simulations of a particular topic or concept, quizzes, games, and other activities to build, support, and extend science learning. Teachers can also find ready-to-go IWB lessons. The BBC Schools site has online simulations for ages 5 to 11. Here, students follow a simple set of directions to witness the results of a changing variable. For example, students can vary the amount of water a plant receives and watch it grow or pluck a guitar string lightly versus intensely while altering the length of the string to hear the differences in the sounds. PhET Interactive Simulations has online activities for older students to explore the concepts of energy, plate tectonics, and molecular science, among other topics. Molecular Workbench has information, online journals, and interactive simulations related to life and physical sciences. Teachers and students may also build their own simulations. Teachers can have students participate in virtual labs by searching for the topic of interest, such as frog dissection or chemical bonding, and the words *virtual lab*.

Digital lab equipment is no longer accessible only by scientists in professional lab settings. Students, too, may take advantage of digital lab equipment in their very own classrooms. Tools, such as digital microscopes, digital scales, digital thermometers, digital oscilloscopes, digital pH meters and voltage meters, digital calipers, soil and water testing kits, incubators, DNA testing kits, portable weather stations, any tools requiring batteries or electricity to function, and solar-powered devices, are available. Additionally, the graphing calculators mentioned earlier have attachments, such as a CBR device, which measures motion, and temperature probes to extend their use. By attaching these tools to graphing calculators, students may apply mathematical concepts as they conduct scientific investigations and make observations of the world around them.

Did you know that many digital measurement tools, such as decibel readers, can be downloaded and used as apps? Before searching through online catalogs and spending precious financial resources on products and tools, check your app store for free resources.

Educational publishing companies are coming out with digital science learning programs. For schools with one-to-one technology or for schools looking to advance their science, technology, engineering, and mathematics (STEM) programs, these are 21st century viable options for schools to pursue. These programs include tutorials, instructional interactive videos, simulation-based activities, online journals, record keeping, and quizzes. Schools without one-to-one technology may be interested in these dynamic programs on a limited basis to challenge students in science and extend their knowledge. Students who have a strong understanding of the science concepts in their grade level may benefit from some independent learning using these digital instructional programs.

Let us not forget the instant connectivity technology offers students. To teach students how scientists collaborate, why not allow them to collaborate with a scientist? Teachers have many options to bring the world of science right into their classrooms. They can join science chat rooms or blogs, pose questions on "Ask a Scientist" websites, watch live scientists in action via real-time video streams, or engage in a conversation with a scientist through video chatting. All of these help build students' understanding of what a scientist is and what he or she does. Teachers can tap local resources, such as engineers, lab technicians, meteorologists, and even plumbers and electricians, who use scientific processes and concepts on a daily basis. These local professionals may be willing to record the work they do on video to share with students. During a live chat, instant messaging session, or even through email, they can answer any student questions about the science involved in their work.

Teachers and students can also participate in online collaborative science-related projects. Collaboration is one of the 4 Cs of 21st century skills (see Chapter 1). Additionally, collaboration is one expectation embedded within the Next Generation Science Standards (NGSS). Cornell University (2014), through their Center for Teaching Excellence, has posted critical information related to the value and use of student collaboration in schools. They state, "Research shows that educational experiences that are active, social, contextual, engaging, and student-owned lead to deeper learning" (Teaching Ideas, Engaging Students).

The Center for Innovation in Engineering and Science Education (CIESE) website lists several online collaboration projects classrooms can join. These activities provide students with opportunities to engage in global data collection on miscellaneous science topics. This helps students understand the value collaboration has on scientists' work as they conduct experiments, compare results, and reach conclusions.

Technology Integration in Social Studies

In addition to math and science, social studies concepts and topics are enhanced with technology. In the digital age, students are no longer limited to reading about history, economics, geography, and civics. Online applications provide many opportunities for students to be active learners with these subjects.

For example, teachers can use online mapping programs to teach geography concepts and map skills. Students can type in their address and map a route to a nearby park. Students can find historical landmarks; identify local geographical features and areas, such as parks and lakes, and global features, such as mountains, oceans, countries, and national forests; and calculate distances and estimate travel times by various modes of transportation. Teachers can have students use online mapping programs as one part of a larger "Tour Our State" research project, wherein students plan a five-day family vacation to various landmarks and points of interest around their state, including travel times to and from each location.

Taking students to historical points of interest brings the imagined world of place and time into reality. For schools cutting back on field trips, virtual field trips abound on the Internet. Classes can visit historical landmarks, historical buildings, and living history museums. Online, students can learn about local history and lore by visiting the area's historical society website. These sites vary from city to city, but they generally include a thorough history of the area along with interesting facts and information, photos of the area from the past, firsthand accounts of historical events, and other stories and folklore.

Reviewing and analyzing primary sources is an essential part of the social studies curriculum. The use of these types of documents is also part of the Common Core State Standards for English Language Arts (2010). Publishing companies provide access to these resources for a fee. Teachers who want to add more primary source documents into their curriculum can access websites, such as the National Archives and Records Administration and the Library of Congress, which hold a variety of primary source documents on various topics of interest. For example, at the Library of Congress website, students can preview a digital file of the actual letter Thomas Jefferson wrote to Congress secretly requesting funding for the Lewis and Clark expedition. The site includes an image of the actual letter as well as a text-based summary of the letter that is readable and printable. In addition to offering a glimpse into real historical documents, primary source websites sometimes offer education or teacher links to provide outlines, lesson ideas, activities, and summaries to help make planning the use of these documents easier for teachers.

Teachers can also find online games and interactive simulations to teach economics, history, geography, and civics. Games provide fun learning activities to reinforce facts and information. Simulations provide digital settings in historical or social studies–based contexts for students to think critically about a particular situation, act according to their knowledge and understanding of the information, and apply their reasoning skills. For example, at the Colonial Williamsburg website, young students can play a game matching up Colonial-era historic establishments with the appropriate skilled tradesman or craftsman signs. Older elementary school students can participate in a National Geograhic simulation to learn about the Lewis and Clark expedition. Middle and high school students can follow an economics-based simulation at Energyville, where they make decisions about the energy mix of a virtual city and discover the economic impacts of their decisions.

Teachers can also use game-like activities as unit reviews. Teachers can find *Jeopardy* templates online and build a review game. Other options include mimicking other popular television fact-based programs such as *Are You Smarter Than a Fifth Grader?* and *Who Wants to Be a Millionaire?* With a small upfront time investment, teachers can save and have these games on hand for future classes, making simple changes as needed to match changing standards, content, and student needs.

Technology Integration in Art, Music, and Physical Education

Technology is not exclusively in the domain of literacy and content-area teachers. Students enjoy joining the digital age in their art, music, and physical education classes as well. All teachers, regardless of what they teach, can find lesson resources, program resources, and videos to enhance their instruction.

For art teachers, the Museum of Modern Art website has images, games, activities, and lesson plans. The ArtBabble website contains videos of art-related topics, narrated by artists and experts in various fields of art. Teachers can search by theme, medium, period, style, and other categories to find just the right video to teach a particular art concept.

For music teachers, Incredibox is an online music-making site that features simple drag-and-drop technology for students to build music with beats, accompaniments, choruses, and voice threads. Elementary school students no longer need to bang on drums to experiment with rhythm. Now they can access Monkey Machine, an online program that allows students to experiment with tempo, rhythm, and beats. Music teachers wanting to make connections with the science behind music and sounds can provide exploration time on the online interactive exhibits of the Exploratorium titled "Science of Music." Here, students choose an online exhibit and interact with the components to make harmonious music and experiment with sounds and rhythms. They can also learn about the science behind sound by watching videos and reading interactive responses to sound-related questions. Classics for Kids is an online resource, teaching young students about classical music. The site is sponsored by Cincinnati Public Radio and offers information about instruments, composers, and musical terms, in addition to providing lesson plans for teachers. ArtsEdge is sponsored by the Kennedy Center. It includes activities, information, lessons, podcasts, and other valuable teaching tools to teach music and culture.

Michelle Davis (2008) explains how schools are combining exercise and gaming (called *exergaming*) to encourage movement in our technologically driven society. Gaming systems provide supplemental equipment for students to perform actions to make images on the screen run, jump, kick, and dance. The use of dance video games and simulation games where gamers take on the role of an action hero require movement and coordination, and provide cardiovascular workouts. Davis cautions educators to be sure to balance new-age technology with traditional activity: "Traditional sports that promote coordination, teamwork, and intense exercise shouldn't fall by the wayside" (para. 9). A Coach's Eye supports instructional form, whether students are playing basketball, volleyball, or another sport. This software allows coaches and gym teachers to video record their students swinging, jumping, kicking, or throwing in any sport. Then the software analyzes the form and offers suggestions for improvement. Users can also compare the recorded players' actions against others, or watch videos of others engaged in a particular sport. This program puts the benefit of professional coaches and players into the palms of teachers' hands.

Technology Integration in Media and Research

The National Technology Standards for students (see Chapter 1) include a category in research and information. In essence, students should be able to "gather, evaluate, and use information" for some intended purpose (ISTE, Standards, Standards for Students). Likewise, Common Core State Standards Writing Standards 7, 8, and 9 require students to write research reports, with Standard 8 specifically requiring the use of digital sources.

Using the Internet to search, locate, and use websites and fact pages to gather reliable information for a research project is a common technology integration in media and research. While classroom teachers may also assign research projects to their students as part of a comprehensive study of a particular topic, media teachers have the advantage of teaching students *how* to conduct searches that yield reliable and appropriate results. One online filter to help with this is EBSCO (Elton B. Stephens Co.). This site eliminates unwanted websites from students' searches and brings them only to sites that directly support their inquiries. Another useful tool when teaching students about research is the interactive research map assembled and published online by the Kentucky Virtual Library. Here, students follow the game-board-like interactive online visual to learn about each step in the research process. The engaging graphics and simple explanations are very useful for both teachers and students who are at the beginning stages of conducting research projects.

The Common Core State Standards Writing Standard 6 also requires students to use digital means to publish and produce writing, as well as "interact and collaborate with others" (corestandards.org).

Using Technology in Early Childhood Programs

Early childhood teachers are not exempt from the potential benefits technology offers their students when effectively integrated into their programs. Computers provide young learners the opportunity to interact with shapes, images, and technology as they explore and make sense of the world around them. Preschool-aged students are likely already armed with computer basics that can easily be utilized in the classroom. For example, a three-year-old child might be able to change the background (or wallpaper) on a personal computer. Another three-year-old might be able to use his or her parent's smartphone to take pictures and instantly email them to Grandma. This background knowledge lays the groundwork for early childhood teachers. Robyn Zevenbergen (2007) refers to these children as "digital natives" (19). Because of the instant media access, digital toys, and electronic components in the home and everything in between, preschool teachers should take care to address both "the types and amount of access to computers children have in their early childhood settings" (23).

Preschool teachers can use developmentally appropriate software and websites with young learners, and ensure a safe environment for students to use the programs. Students can learn to count, match letter sounds, and match letters to pictures. Interactive features on tablets and whiteboards allow students to interact with software programs and games, dragging and tracing to complete a task. Students can hear stories read aloud, and create their own displays of digital pictures to show examples of numbers or letters. With a knowledgeable staff, integrating technology into the prekindergarten classroom can be as easy as A–B–C.

This is not to say that early childhood programs should be entirely digital. In an interview by Early Childhood Today, Dr. Bruce Perry, an internationally recognized authority on brain development and children in crisis, cautions, *Children need real-life experiences with real people to truly benefit from available technologies. Technologies should be used to enhance curriculum and experiences for children. Children have to have an integrated and well-balanced set of experiences to help them grow into capable adults that can handle social-emotional interactions as well as develop their intellectual abilities.* (Moore Kneas and Perry, para. 12)

Along with computer integration, early childhood programs should continue to invite students to explore and learn through songs, movement, and tactile activities to maintain a balanced, appropriate, and comprehensive learning program.

Conclusion

Technology integration spans all subjects and all grade levels. Educators who teach content-area subjects can find and use valuable learning tools for computers, personal tablets, and mobile learning devices. Likewise, special technology equipment, such as digital stopwatches and microscopes, helps provide a comprehensive learning environment. Students can collaborate electronically to complete special content area–based projects and use presentation software to meet the expectations of the CCSS with regard to creating and publishing student writing. With all of these actions merging into every aspect of students' learning experiences, regardless of the topic, schools can use the digital tools needed to broaden students' depth of knowledge and help them apply essential technology skills necessary for today's 21st century learners.

Reflect and Respond

1. In what ways have you integrated technology into one or more of the content areas that you teach?

2. What are additional ways you might integrate technology into one or more of the content areas you teach?

3. What instructional objectives will this technology support?

4. How do you think your students will respond to the use of this technology in the classroom? Explain.

Chapter 5

Online Applications to Extend Learning and Thinking

Life in the 21st century is dominated by technology, especially online applications. From reading blogs to interacting through social media to hunting high and low for the perfect activity or instructional resource, how much time would you estimate you spend online? What about texting? The Internet is an integral part of our lives. We likely go online every day for something. From online shopping to checking out what's trending, the Internet holds a world of resources and activities.

Flipped Classrooms

Schools are in varying places of adoption and implementation of the popular one-to-one initiative, which provides a personal computer, tablet, or other device to each student. Some schools have every student connected all day, every day, while other schools may have just one or two grade levels or one or two classes connected to technology day in and day out. Still other schools may have a shared computer lab, only have a single computer per classroom, or some other combination. The one-to-one initiative, however, supports the idea of flipping classrooms because students have easy access to digital lessons.

In a flipped classroom, the teacher video records (e.g., live or through a slide show presentation) a lesson in advance of it being covered in class. The viewing of this lesson is then assigned to students as homework. The idea is that when students arrive in class the next day, they are armed with the necessary vocabulary and background knowledge to be able to utilize class time for the application of the content. As a result, the teacher is free to spend class time clearing up misconceptions and engaging students in an applicable activity or written assignment, rather than direct instruction.

Initial research on the topic of the flipped classroom is promising. In an article posted to "District Administration," Clintondale High School in Clinton Township, Michigan had shown a reduced failure rate among freshmen math students (from 44 to 13 percent after one year of implementation), and a 10 percent increase in juniors' math achievement scores (Finkel 2012). Bryan Goodwin and Kirsten Miller (2013) also reflect on promising results. In a nonscientific study, about two-thirds of teachers surveyed reported an increase in their students' test scores, particularly with students in Advanced Placement (AP) classes, and with students with special needs. These same teachers also acknowledged an increase in students' attitudes, and nearly all committed to a flipped learning environment during the subsequent school year.

Teachers who use flipped classrooms claim it maximizes time during the school day because they devote more time to applying the concept or skill than teaching it (Sams and Bergmann 2013). Students can bring their questions to class while teachers can quickly assess student understanding. As a result, the teacher can address misconceptions or difficulties grasping the content at the onset of the lesson as opposed to the middle of it. This also enables the teacher to establish follow-ups with small groups of students more easily in the time allotted. For example, if a teacher knows that five students tend to struggle with new or even reviewed math skills, he or she may differentiate the work assignment for the lesson to best meet the needs of these students and work with them while other students work independently or in collaborative groups to extend their learning.

With a flipped classroom, the Internet is required for teachers to post their tutorials, presentations, videos, and podcasts, and for students to view the materials. School and district servers are likely not suited for emailing such large files. Thus, teachers use online, free or subscription, open-source, cloud-based learning management programs, such as Moodle, Edmodo, or LaunchPad, to post their lessons.

It is important to acknowledge that not all schools are involved in one-to-one initiatives, and teachers cannot guarantee that all students have Internet access beyond the school's walls. Alternate pathways can be provided. For example, if teachers have access to a computer lab, they can schedule time for students to watch the week's lessons during a portion of the day or class period. Although this does not necessarily give students access to the lessons throughout the week, they can pause to take notes or jot down questions to ask later in class. Another option is to burn the recorded lessons onto a disk for students to watch at home. There is some cost incurred with this option, but it is minimal when used only for students who need it.

Something else to consider is that video recorded lessons do not all need to be made by classroom teachers. Students can be assigned an online tutorial on YouTube, TeacherTube, Khan Academy, O_2 Learn, National Geographic, or PBS LearningMedia. Alternately, students can access online tutorials provided by their own textbook series since many textbook companies provide relevant and meaningful digital resources to students and teachers in conjunction with the print material. These resources can be valuable time-savers for teachers wanting to implement the flipped classroom. Still another option is to have students spend time making their own video lessons for teachers to use during subsequent school years. For example, instead of reading about or listening to a lesson on story structure, a small group of students can create and publish a video or podcast about it. As part of the learning process, students can act out each part of the story's structure using a literature selection they read in class that year.

Distance Learning and Virtual School

Returning for an advanced degree, adding-on to state certification, and continued professional development courses through a virtual school is a popular vehicle for many working professionals. These online programs are popular since they are asynchronous and can be accessed anytime, day or night. They provide teachers flexible timelines to complete the work at their own pace within their particular schedule. Distance learning or virtual school programs (also called eLearning) are sometimes just as popular and just as appropriate for students.

Technology ushers in fundamental structural changes that can be integral to achieving significant improvements in productivity. Used to support both teaching and learning, technology infuses classrooms with digital learning tools, such as computers and handheld devices; expands course offerings, experiences, and learning materials; supports learning twenty-four hours a day, seven days a week; builds 21st century skills; increases student engagement and motivation; and accelerates learning. Technology also has the power to transform teaching by ushering in a new model of connected teaching. This model links teachers to their students and to professional content, resources, and systems to help them improve their own instruction and personalize learning.

Online learning opportunities and the use of open educational resources and other technologies can increase educational productivity by accelerating the rate of learning; reducing costs associated with instructional materials or program delivery; and better utilizing teacher time. (The U.S. Department of Education 2014, "Use of Technology in Teaching and Learning")

Virtual or distance learning programs may be used in several different ways to support the efforts of teachers and schools to educate students. Some students attend virtual school full time. This means that all of their coursework is completed and all of their requirements are met through virtual classes. They do not attend a physical school campus, although their district may allow them to participate in sports or special programs, such as art or band, on campus. These full-time schools may be operated through a state's department of education or through a particular school district.

Another option for students is to participate in a *blended curriculum* program where they attend virtual classes on a part-time basis. This option is advantageous to students who need advanced or remedial courses, or who wish to take electives that would not otherwise "fit" into their schedule due to scheduling conflicts, teacher shortages, or other coursework restrictions. For example, a middle-school student may have demonstrated that he or she is prepared for algebra II, a course not provided by the middle school. Rather than wait until high school, this student could attend an online institute, either during the school day on campus or before or after school hours. Another advantage to part-time virtual school attendance is that students may take courses at any time from any computer with Internet access. For students who live and attend school in rural areas where coursework options may be limited, virtual school classes provide them with educational opportunities on par with those available to their urban and suburban counterparts.

A popular online instructional tool that equips students to become independent learners and thinkers is engaging in WebQuests, which was developed in early 1995 by Bernie Dodge at San Diego State University (WebQuest.org 2007). Since its inception, tens of thousands of teachers have embraced WebQuests as not only effective uses of the Internet but effective ways to develop 21st century thinking skills in their students.

WebQuests involve student collaborative teams to complete a series of tasks that collectively fulfill an overall objective or goal. Each student tackles one part of the project. Then the group members assemble their parts into one complete project. Explicit, clear modeling is instrumental to a successful WebQuest. It begins with an introduction, moves on to the tasks, explains the process for completion, includes an evaluation system, reaches a conclusion, and offers credits. WebQuests may also include links to resources, such as websites, podcasts, documents, forms, or other essential project components. Although the project is introduced and delivered to students online and the students follow the steps to complete the project both as a group and as individuals, the teacher oversees the project, assisting with research as needed and ensuring that students are on track to finish on time.

WebQuests are authentic and motivating instructional tasks to use with students. They set clear purposes for learning and put students in charge of their own learning. Of course, teachers need to provide adequate access to computers with Internet access and online resources so that students can complete the project assigned to them. In schools that do not have the one-to-one advantage, the teacher may introduce the project to the whole class using a projector and then schedule lab time for students to do their online work. Additionally, each group may be offered computer time within the classroom on certain days at certain times to conduct their research. Alternately, the groups may assign the online work to students who have Internet access at home, and then use the class period to share information and combine their efforts to complete the tasks. This latter suggestion may not allow equitable access to all students for the primary purpose of WebQuests: online learning. However, for teachers facing limited computer use, it is an option.

Interactive Games, Activities, and Simulations

Interactive games, interactive activities, and online simulations were mentioned in Chapter 4 as powerful tools to help students learn the facts and information they need to know, as well as apply concepts and ideas in novel situations. Because they are popular with students, and they effectively reinforce skills students need to master, interactive activities bear mentioning here again as an effective use of online programs.

Games

Robert Marzano (2010) has researched the effects games have on student learning. He has discovered that, "on average, using academic games in the classroom is associated with a 20 percentile point gain in student achievement." He considers this to be a "relatively strong finding." Additionally, the benefits of gaming in the classroom include increased memory, class performance, social benefits, and improving the transfer of learning (Salies 2002, para. 2).

When gaming, students use skills and knowledge to win something, accomplish a goal, or reach a desired level. For example, students might have to complete a set of analogies to earn points. Games have several advantages for student learning. They provide engaging, motivating, safe opportunities for students to practice skills they typically need to begin to complete higher-level tasks. Academic game sites usually offer a range of task levels so that students can feel successful and build on their skill set. Games can require analytical thinking, problem solving, planning, and strategy adjustment in fast-paced situations. The goals of games are clear, and students understand the expectations and strive to accomplish them with their academic prowess. Some games provide progress-monitoring options for teachers, so they can monitor student progress as they work their way through the tasks. Popular online learning game resources may be found at PBS Kids, Scholastic, and Funbrain.

Activities

Activities are similar to games, except students don't really win anything—there's no reward at the end of the skill drill. Students might simply see a score or move on to a more challenging set of tasks. Activities tend to be interactive and offer immediate feedback regarding correct and incorrect answers. They might include interactive word searches, polls, quizzes, or drag-and-drop activities. Popular activity sites include ReadWriteThink and National Geographic Kids. Teachers can also find a slew of ready-to-go interactive whiteboard (IWB) activities. The use of this technology tool is more thoroughly discussed in Chapter 6.

Simulations

Simulations take students through a fictional yet real-life situation with the purpose of reaching a specific goal. They offer students practical, real-world application of knowledge and skills to accomplish an objective. Classroom simulations can positively impact student learning when they are firmly linked to content and learning objectives (Wedig 2010). For example, students might manipulate the temperature of an environment or hunt prey as a predator to keep an ecosystem balanced. Simulations are helpful for both one-to-one classrooms and for classrooms with just one computer. In one-to-one situations, students can work independently or in pairs to engage in the simulation. In classrooms with just one computer, the simulation can be used with the whole class. Student group leaders can converse with their teams and write the desired next step(s) on a whiteboard. The teacher can then act on the most popular choice as the simulation progresses.

Teachers can use purchased games, activities, and resources to provide simulated tasks to students. Alternately, they can access the Internet, find a simulation pertinent to a current topic of study, and set students to their task. One such simulation is called Oregon Trail, which has evolved over the years from its original computer game format. Simulations are generally specific to the content areas. Teachers interested in finding a grade- and topic-appropriate simulation can use their favorite search engine to search for the topic title and the word *simulations* (or variations such as *simulations for kids* or *simulations for middle school*).

Blogs and Social Networking

Many teachers agree: learning requires interaction and communication. Today's commonplace use of technology to stay connected, including social media, "has widened the dimensions of the available spaces for the social component of learning" (Arora 2013, para. 1). Blogs and social networking are part of everyday life. They permeate every facet of our world from business to politics (Stokes 2011). Students today (and some adults) have a hard time keeping their electronic devices put away for any length of time. They want to be in constant contact with others. Texting today seems as common as talking. The advantage is that the conversation remains quiet and secretive as long as the people texting have their devices on mute. However, as Justin Reich from the Harvard Graduate School of Education reminds us (in a blog sponsored by Common Sense Education), "Even if remarkably high percentages of students report using technology, it doesn't mean they know what they are doing" (Stokes 2011, "Social media are transforming our world—education needs to change, too"). Instead of banishing instant communication altogether, teachers and schools can channel the students' desire to stay connected through more educational channels.

Virtual learning is quickly becoming the norm in classrooms. Schools that have one-to-one technology may use "virtual classrooms" to post and access curriculum material and assignments. Additionally, they typically encourage students to collaborate with one another. These cloud-based classrooms provide real-time learning through a digital platform. Gaggle is one online resource that allows students to safely connect with each other online through both email and blogs.

Using the Internet for Blogging

Blogs have historically been used for personal use; however, there is a purposeful place for them in education. The term *blog* is actually short for *weblog*. Someone who starts a blog has something to say, and he or she wants to share it with the world. These are the diaries of the 21st Century. By posting regularly to a blog site, the author may easily transmit this information to anyone who wants to access the blog. Readers who come to like a particular blog will return time and time again to see what is new and what is trending, or gain more up-to-date information from the author. As a new post is made, the previous posts remain archived and continuously accessible. Some blogs allow for readers to post their thoughts, reactions, or ideas below the blog entry in the comments section, making the blog page interactive.

Blogs are useful to classrooms. They can provide information for parents and offer an informal collaborative discussion forum for parents (and students) to reflect and respond to topics, tasks, and procedures. Teachers can post information about assignments or current topics (including links to videos and other media), and students can reflect on their learning publically (rather than privately in a response journal). These uses definitely increase collaboration and communication among all stakeholders: teachers, parents, and students.

According to Richard E. Ferdig and Kaye D. Trammell (2004), there are four benefits of student blogging. They are:

- students become subject-matter experts;
- student interest and ownership in learning increases;
- students are given legitimate chances to participate; and
- students are provided with opportunities for exposure to diverse perspectives, both within and outside of the classroom.

Edublogs is an online resource for teachers wanting to use blogs with students. This organization believes that blogs increase student engagement and help students maintain ownership of and take pride in their own learning. The Edublogs website offers these tips for teachers wanting to start a blog in the classroom:

- Set clear guidelines and expectations.
- Teach students how to leave meaningful, quality comments.
- Teach students to edit their posts before posting them online.
- Use the posts to engage and motivate students, and improve reading and thinking skills.

Teachers wanting to try out classroom blogs may start by using Edublogs, Blogger (affiliated with Google), SchoolRack, or Teacher Blog It. Teachers should do their research first and make sure the blog resource is age appropriate and offers everything their students will need to successfully publish a blog. Take a tour of the website. Be sure it meets your expectations and is easy enough to use, even for beginners.

Using the Internet for Social Networking for Kids

Many schools caution teachers to stay away from using the leading social networking sites. Schools and/or school districts may even block access to popular sites. However, teachers should be aware that there are a few kid-friendly, safe social networking sites that exist solely for the purpose of allowing students to interact on a global scale without the common concern of maintaining a controlled environment. Sites such as Kidzworld and Yoursphere offer alternatives to unchecked social networking and have links, activities, information, and highlights that interest young students and young teenagers. Students can post comments or reflections related to classroom activities and assignments during school hours, as part of their nightly homework, or simply for fun. Teachers across districts or schools can have students collaborate on projects, using social networking to post websites or other links to information. Teachers can check in with students regarding lengthier assignments, posting questions related to the progress students are making and the challenges they are facing. These sites are viable options for teachers interested in having students meet the national and state writing standards requiring the use of technology to produce and publish writing in addition to collaborating with other students.

Related to social networking is the idea of using video chatting. This online system connects students and classrooms in real time to other students, classrooms, and field experts. This 21st century version of pen pals expands classroom walls, widens students' perspectives, and brings a new dimension to teaching and learning. A *TIME* magazine online article by Olivia B. Waxman (2012) explains how a third-grade teacher, Amy Rosenstein, uses video chatting to bring world geography to life for her students. She conducts interviews of potential participants beforehand and explains the purpose for the chat. She sets up the session, and students are instantly transported to another city, state, or even country in the world to experience art, history, and culture. Video chatting is useful for bringing in guest speakers or for allowing students to collaborate globally on a curriculum-related project. It serves to broaden their education.

Websites

Where would we be without our favorite websites? Social networking sites aside, perhaps you rely on online television listings, movie review sites, daily national or local news, newspaper sites, mapping or GPS sites, or entertainment sites, such as a quote of the day or SAT problem of the day. We all have our favorites as users of online technology. Educators are no different. Teachers can pull in information for myriad uses, expanding students' access to information and helping them make connections among content. For example, a teacher might start off with a look at TIME for Kids online to check into current events before beginning the day's lesson in social studies. Another teacher may find value in having students play an online logic game as a bell-ringer activity.

A *bell-ringer* is a short activity for students to complete while the teacher takes attendance.

Additionally, educators might bookmark their favorite professional sites, such as lesson plan links, resource links, and educator social networking sites and blogs. Websites are one part of what the U.S. Department of Education, Office of Educational Technology calls a "Universal Design for Learning" (UDL). The compilation of neuroscience research concludes that there are three general types of learning: learning what, learning how, and learning why. Website usage "represent[s] information through a much richer mix of media types. This allows the integration of media and representations to illustrate, explain, or explore complex ideas and phenomena, such as interactive visualizations of data in earth and environmental sciences, chemistry, or astronomy. Technology can help learners explore phenomena at extreme spatial or temporal scales through simulation and modeling tools. This opens up many domains and ways of learning that were formerly impossible or impractical" (2010, under "Factual Knowledge").

Teachers might also be interested in having students design, construct, and maintain a classroom website filled with academic information, classroom information, relevant links to other websites, pictures of classroom happenings, a classroom calendar with current events, and more. Once teachers demonstrate how to update the site, they can assign this task to students on a rotating weekly basis. There are numerous benefits to enlisting student assistance. First, students can take pride in their participation. Second, teachers can feel confident that they are meeting one of the state or national standards. Finally, parent activity might surge when he or she knows their child (and their child's classmates) created the information.

Websites also offer unique publishing features that students can use to enhance their written work. For example, Blabberize is a Flash-based site that allows students to make pictures talk. Voki is a site where students can choose an avatar, and then have their avatar complete classwork for them, such as summarize a section of text or explain a curriculum-related process.

We access and use websites for a variety of reasons. As teachers, we can utilize these tools to expand our thinking, planning, and instruction in creative, thoughtful, and meaningful ways.

Research

Using technology to support reference and research skills was first discussed in Chapter 1. The Internet has many valuable, reliable sites that teachers can use to support student learning. Students are naturally curious and ask many questions. Researching answers to their questions is one way to develop their critical thinking skills and develop their background knowledge. For example, say that students are curious about dust devils, a topic they recently came across in their literature selection. This may be a familiar concept for students who live in the desert Southwest; however, for students in the Appalachian Mountains, dust devils are likely a foreign idea. When the teacher's explanation is not sufficient, students can go online and find information, pictures, and maybe even a video clip to gain a better understanding.

As 21st century information seekers, teachers play a crucial role in the development and honing of effective research skills. They can assign individual or group research projects, or use websites to teach students how to search for, find, and use reliable sites (and reference them appropriately).

The Internet is filled with information, and the following sites might help narrow the focus for students when they set off to find information on their own:

- Association for Library Service to Children (ALSC), http://www.ala.org/alsc

- HowStuffWorks, http://www.howstuffworks.com

- KidsClick!, http://www.kidsclick.org

Furthermore, students might use some of the safe social networking sites discussed earlier in this chapter as places to pose questions and gather information from their peer group. Another option is to reach out to experts in specific fields for information. Students might find a blog written by an astronaut, musician, or archaeologist.

Apps

Apps can be a useful and supportive resource in the digital classroom. *Apps* (short for online application or applet) are small software files intended for a specific purpose and are usually downloaded and used on small personal devices, such as smartphones or tablets. Some are offered for a small fee; others are free. Apps are available for various operating systems and devices. Teachers (and students) with personal smartphones or tablets may use these resources in their classrooms to support teaching and learning. They can be used in multiple settings, such as whole group, small group, or individually.

Do educational iPad apps positively effect learning? According to University of Southern California Professor Michelle Riconscente, they do. GameDesk conducted a study on the Motion Math app designed for elementary school-aged children to work on fractions. *Among the main findings were that fractions knowledge increased an average of 15 percent, and participants gained confidence in their fractions ability and reported liking fractions more after playing the game* (2013, para. 1).

The Internet is filled with apps for students of all ages and for every subject. Like websites, useful classroom apps are too numerous and too widespread to mention by name here. Teachers wanting to use more online applications in a wider variety of contexts can use other teachers' and experts' suggestions as a starting point by following their websites or blogs, or by conducting an online search for a particular app. Teachers can use apps, like software, to teach particular topics and concepts. Teachers can assign specific tasks to students or groups of students. Since apps generally provide instant feedback and correction as students complete a task, they may correct misconceptions

iPad Apps for Classrooms

- **Amazing Alex:** Provides physics-based thinking games
- **BookLeveler:** Finds the "just right" book anytime, anywhere
- **Flashcards:** Creates practice flash cards for vocabulary or math problems
- **Popplet:** Creates virtual concept maps
- **ShowMe:** Turns a tablet into a tutorial recorder
- **Singapore Math:** Offers interactive problem solving
- **Toontastic:** Walks students through story writing process
- **Sphere:** Takes students on virtual visits anywhere in the world

immediately, and practice new skills appropriately. Teachers can also assign homework practice on the app. To hold students accountable for their practice, the teacher may require students to post a summary of what happened when they used the app. As with websites, teachers should try out the app before class to be sure it helps them and their students reach the desired instructional objective and is easy to use.

Videos

They say a picture is worth a thousand words. So, what is a video file worth? For students who lack personal experiences to bring meaning to new learning, the Internet is filled with appropriate, tactful, and meaningful videos that teachers can use. These valuable resources build students' background knowledge, demonstrate a process or concept, or show students participating in an event or procedure. According to Douglas Fisher and Nancy Frey (2011), "There is tremendous value in combining words and images to show students how the content of our disciplines is understood outside school walls" (5). Teachers who use videos can help students make new connections between related curriculum topics. Videos can bring the outside world in and demonstrate the relevance and application of what students are learning. Videos also tap into various learning modalities, a requirement of state and national standards. Teachers can use videos to teach critical thinking skills by having them compare the essential message from a text to the essential message from a video about the topic.

Using videos is an important and helpful means to linking complex, abstract concepts to concrete examples and illustrations. They also level the educational playing field, providing common experiences for all students, regardless of background knowledge.

Possible Uses of Video in the Classroom

- Go on virtual field trips, such as to the San Diego Zoo, Lincoln Memorial, or a power plant.
- Provide global learning opportunities.
- Demonstrate processes and procedures (e.g., science experiments) that are not feasible to do in class.
- Bring classic literature and stories to life.

As with any instructional tool, teachers should abide by common sense best practices when incorporating video into the classroom.

- Preview the content to be sure it is appropriate for students.

- Connect the video to instructional learning objectives.

- Provide an outline, list of questions, or other accountability tool, such as a graphic organizer or vocabulary words, for students to complete as evidence of learning.

- Pause as needed to allow for class discussion and time for students to respond in writing to the information.

- Follow up with critical thinking questions and summarization activities to demonstrate to students that the information in the video is important and connected to learning.

Video tools need not be view-only. For example, students might collaborate to create a video presentation about idiomatic expressions or multiplying fractions. This type of project requires students to plan, organize, develop, synthesize, edit, revise, and publish independent, creative writing projects. For schools with advanced technology capabilities, students can use hardware and software to film, and then crop and shift sections of film to achieve the desired effects. Schools without advanced technology may have students plan and organize a simpler project, and then film it using whatever hardware is available, including smartphones with video-capturing capabilities. Students may not have the advantage of the film-editing process, but they will still have to maneuver through the writing process to complete their project. Using video recording equipment for educational purposes is discussed further in Chapter 6.

Additionally, part of the video publishing process might include students' involvement in community service projects. School grants may require the submission of a video as part of the application process. Local or national companies may give away school-related equipment by having a video submission contest. Likewise, students may participate in a public service announcement (PSA) contest put on by the state department of education or other government agency for a chance to win various prizes and awards. These types of projects show students the importance of community service while simultaneously offering an authentic application of writing skills.

Conclusion

The Internet's resources for teachers and students are infinite. Its usefulness as an instructional tool is limited only by the creativity of the teachers who access it. The Internet provides a unique learning platform for 21st century learners. They can use it to access information quickly, connect to others instantaneously, and post and publish individual or collaborative projects. As long as teachers have a topic to teach, the Internet has an instructional resource to connect students in the classroom to the world around them.

Reflect and Respond

1. What do you believe is the most valuable use of the Internet to enhance and support the learning experience? How have you used the Internet for this purpose?

2. What is one use of the Internet that you have not attempted before that you would be willing to try with students? How will you connect this idea to an instructional objective?

3. How might you evaluate the effectiveness of the use of the Internet in your classroom?

4. What challenges do you face using the Internet with students? What ideas do you have to overcome these challenges?

Chapter 6

Moving Beyond Computers

Technology moves faster than... well, faster than you can read this. The hardware options available for teachers and students today are more numerous than anyone could have imagined just ten years ago. The disadvantage to rapidly changing hardware is that it is often outdated before it even has a chance to be broken in. Cell phones are the epitome of this idea. It seems as if an updated phone is launched every day. Carriers have new and improved plans, phone companies have new and improved features, online services have new and improved apps—it never ends.

Education, however, usually does not move as quickly. Schools may have new and improved technology every so often, but more likely, they are working with the same technology (e.g., hardware systems) that they had a year, three years, or even five years ago. Teachers learn to do what they can with what they have. The chapters leading up to this one have explored instructional strategies, activities, and resources to which most schools have access, particularly in the area of software applications and online resources. This chapter focuses on all the "toys" out there—hardware that makes learning fun and teaching exciting and fresh. Financial resource options for purchasing these are listed in Chapter 1. Even if a school must go without, it is interesting and inspiring to know what is available to 21st century students.

Whole-Class Hardware Systems

Computers are only useful when they have all of the specifications, programs, Internet connectivity, and printing capabilities that teachers need to perform the tasks required. Even in one-computer classrooms, the teacher and students can benefit from the machine's resourcefulness.

In addition to this useful tool, schools may have large-scale technology equipment to further support instruction. This section explores the types of hardware that help teachers use computers more effectively in a whole-class setting.

Interactive Whiteboards

Interactive whiteboards (IWBs) work with a computer and projection system. The projector projects computer images onto a special screen, which transforms the images and icons into digital images that may be manipulated on the screen itself. An IWB saves a teacher from having to rely on a computer to demonstrate processes. Instead of sitting behind a desk manipulating the mouse and keyboard, the teacher may use the IWB to manipulate the images at the front of the room. Additionally, students may drag, type, write, and draw on the screen, using the projected images as tangible interactive tools versus intangible stationary images. For example, the teacher may have a list of words for students to sort. Instead of writing them on a regular whiteboard, only to have to rewrite them to sort them, or instead of projecting them from a word-processing document onto an ordinary screen, the words may be typed into an IWBs' software program. Now students can drag and drop the words right on the IWB to sort and classify them. The newly sorted lists may be saved and filed for later use.

IWBs provide several benefits to classrooms. First, they have been proven to increase students' academic performance, especially in the area of mathematics (Kopp 2013, 11). This makes sense, since math is a subject area that requires the manipulation of numbers and symbols. The more readily students can physically manipulate these numbers and symbols, the more likely it is that they conceptually acquire and permanently retain mathematical skills, concepts, and processes. Additionally, IWBs are useful tools for increasing student engagement in the classroom. Since IWBs are interactive, students take on a more active role in their own learning, rather than relying on the teacher to disseminate the information they need to learn. An IWB transforms passive learners into active, engaged learners. Finally, IWBs are part of a sustainable classroom, one that does not require extensive (and expensive) frequent upgrades. An IWB is a device in and of itself, connected to a projector, which is connected to a computer. Even though each of these hardware devices is expensive, they typically do not need regular replacements. So, in the long run, they keep costs down, and they can support and maintain effective instruction for quite some time.

As mentioned, the IWB itself (and the software it uses) can be quite expensive up front. However, technology being what it is, companies are now competing for business. Where there is competition, there are competitive prices and a competitive market. Classrooms are no longer restricted to purchasing one brand. Today, many companies have options available for schools (and businesses) at a variety of price points and with a variety of sizes, features, and options.

The use of an IWB can completely change the structure and function of a classroom. It is indeed a valuable asset to any teacher and his or her group of students in today's digital age.

> An *IWB* can be a valuable instructional tool when the teacher uses virtual manipulatives to illustrate and demonstrate a mathematical process to build conceptual understanding.

Document Cameras

Another useful and cost-effective projection device is the document camera. These tools replace overhead projectors that require clear acetate pages imprinted with text and images. Again, working with the computer and a projection system, the document camera does not require teachers to run special pages in order for students to see the images on the screen. According to the Educational Technology Network (2009), document cameras benefit both visual and tactile learners. They also reduce the cost of making copies, since teachers may use any paper or other flat document exactly as it is to demonstrate a point or to use as a model for instruction. This includes textbooks, printed papers, workbook pages, photos, and diagrams. Additionally, teachers can model how to complete a particular workbook page, worksheet, or graphic organizer simply by placing it under the document camera and writing on the paper. It is also useful for grading.

Posting the answer key or completing it along with students helps give students instant feedback on their work. Document cameras are also helpful for sharing student-written work. Their work can be used in a variety of ways, such as how they approached and solved a math problem, set up a science experiment, or outlined their ideas for a story.

Like IWBs, document cameras have evolved quickly since first arriving in classrooms. There are many makes and models to choose from at all different price points. In addition, some IWB companies have developed their own versions of document cameras that work collaboratively with the IWB. In this instance, the teacher has the benefit of the computer, projector, IWB, and document camera all functioning as a collective unit.

No display timer? No problem! Use a personal smartphone or tablet with a timer function. Place the device under the document camera and start the countdown. Students can always see how much time they have remaining for a specific task.

Wireless Projection

Many classrooms today have at least one computer hooked up to a projection system. Both IWBs and document cameras require the projection of digital displays through an essential piece of classroom hardware: the digital projector. But what if a teacher moves the class to an area of the building without a hardwired connection to the projector? Or what about teachers who want to move about freely in the classroom using wireless technology rather than being locked behind a desk with the hardwired computer system? Teachers (and other professionals) can now download and use an app that allows them to wirelessly connect to a projector from their tablet or other mobile device. They need the capability to wirelessly connect to the projector's network, and then they may launch the projection app and freely display their slide show, website, or other documents without having to connect from one location in the room. This is a valuable tool as schools and classrooms begin to move to one-to-one situations with smaller tablets, or for schools wanting to move away from large, bulky desktop computers to portable technology systems. This app allows teachers to maintain their projection capabilities without the need for hardwired systems. When students with tablets need to share a project, they can simply hook into the projector wirelessly, rather than spend time downloading, uploading, and sending their files to their teacher to use from his or her wired computer station.

Poster Printers

The days of having to make charts, diagrams, and visual displays using tag board and markers are *over*. Teachers can use any computer software program to design and make digital displays. Then they run them through a poster printer, which enlarges the images and text as it prints. This piece of hardware works like a regular printer, but it uses oversized paper. Some poster printers have color ink, which is especially beneficial for diagrams, graphs, charts, and maps. Additionally, poster printers can use paper that may be laminated. By running a document through a poster printer, laminating it, and applying poster tabs or tape that turns any document into a sticky note, teachers can post the visual any time to use as needed. Thanks to technology, teachers are no longer limited to specialized posters that must be ordered. They can run and print personalized documents for any purpose, any time.

There are many uses for color poster printers, spanning various content areas. One way a language arts teacher could use it is when teaching effective essay writing. Teachers can use a word-processing document to type a model essay, and use different colored text or highlight features to identify topic sentences and substantiated claims, specific nouns, strong verbs, or any other literary device they want to call out. The printed poster can then be used as an effective visual model of an essay and its must-have features.

Student Response Systems

Another effective digital tool teachers can employ are student response systems. These handheld devices enable students to submit their answers to projected questions with multiple-choice answers. Once the question is "closed," students can see a graph showing the percentage of students who selected each answer choice along with the actual correct answer. The teacher can use the results to reinforce the skill posed by the question or clarify any misconceptions or misunderstandings.

Marzano Research Laboratory was commissioned by Promethean Ltd. for a second year to study the effects of the use of their interactive whiteboard (IWB) with students. Robert Marzano and Mark Haystead (2010) summarized the study in a final report. In the study, one academic advantage they discovered was the use of the "voting devices" (or student response systems). The study found that the use of student response systems in classrooms that used IWBs increased students' overall achievement by 26 percentile points. Although this particular study was connected to the use of response systems with IWBs, interactive whiteboards are not a necessary piece of technology equipment for classrooms using student response systems.

Many companies produce varied student response systems, leaving the choice of which one to purchase up to individual schools or school districts. A system may work with software already available on the teacher's computer, usually a slide show program. Other systems require the use of that company's software program, which is downloaded onto the teacher's computer. Remote systems vary greatly from one system to the next. Some remotes have only letter responses, limiting the students' responses to one answer choice. Other remotes have both numeric and alphabetical options, allowing students to participate in multiple-choice assessments as well as to "text" answers to fill-in-the-blank and short-answer questions. Some remotes are just that: remotes with button controls. Others have LCD (liquid-crystal display) screens that allow students to preview their responses before submitting them as their final answer selections.

Additionally, these devices save teachers time and reduce the use of consumables. Once teachers have their assessments loaded into the software program, they are there permanently and can be modified from year to year. Teachers do not have to run copies of tests and quizzes. Instead, they may simply display each test question one at a time and have students enter their answer digitally. This allows for instant scoring and score reporting. Teachers can pull up test results and reports instantly. Some systems will even interface with a digital gradebook, linking test scores directly into the teacher's grades. Teachers can monitor, question by question, which students have completed the test items, ensuring that no one skips a question.

Mobile Devices

Society is changing daily, in part due to the rapid advancements in mobile technology. People no longer need to wait to get to work or to get home to log onto their computers to check financial statistics, read and send email, or catch up on office work. Instead, they can use their mobile devices on the go in any location where they can access the Internet. Mobile devices are defined as any handheld device that work wirelessly, using Wi-Fi or a network to connect to the Internet and/or the device's operating system. These devices include tablets, smartphones, and eReaders and are usually more affordable than standard computer systems; however, they require access to an online service provider, which comes with a monthly or annual fee. A recent study found that students who had access to a tablet in their classroom were 6 percent more likely to pass a state reading exam and 8 percent more likely to pass a state writing exam (TeachThought 2012). So it is not surprising that schools are turning to mobile devices when seeking one-to-one capabilities for their students. After all, schools cannot expect students to carry around their own personal computer from class to class, and outfitting each classroom with computer labs would require extensive retrofits to allow for the electrical and hardwired access to the school's server system. Mobile devices, such as tablets, are a cost-effective means of providing technology to every student.

The use of mobile technology in the classroom enables teachers to post lessons, links, and information where students may access them on their own devices. This idea, discussed in Chapter 5, includes cloud storage sites. Additionally, teachers can use cloud storage for students to post their digitally completed assignments. This 21st Century "in basket" removes century-old excuses such as "I left my homework at home" and "My dog ate my homework." Everything is digital; students have access to their assignments from any device by simply logging into their accounts. Popular student assignment collection sites, aside from the ones mentioned earlier, include eBackpack, Box, and Schoology. Some storage sites even allow students to access and revise their postings.

With the availability of mobile devices and the fact that young children use them regularly (Grunwald Associates LLC 2013), teachers need not worry about students fumbling and stumbling to learn a new system for accessing, completing, and posting work. Instead of setting up tangible notebooks, folders, and papers at the start of school, teachers walk their students through the accessing and posting process. Mobile devices become especially valuable when students can access their textbooks digitally, too. Students can significantly reduce the amount of weight they carry around in their backpacks, so an argument can be made that one-to-one schools contribute to the overall health of their students in addition to broadening and strengthening the students' academics.

Schools with limited mobile devices may consider having portable labs. In this situation, the mobile devices are placed on a cart with electronic connections (for easy charging when not in use). The lab is assigned to certain classrooms for a certain time period, or teachers may have the freedom to check out the rolling labs as they need to support instruction. These labs are advantageous for schools that lack adequate space for traditional, dedicated computer labs, but they are not without their drawbacks. Since the labs work wirelessly, they may face security challenges and schools may lack the infrastructure (local and wide area network capacity) to allow so many devices to run simultaneously around the school. Charging time must also be factored into the daily life of the portable devices. They will not last all day in the hands of students, and teachers may find themselves on the tail end of a device's battery life, limiting its use during their scheduled time. This can cause frustration for both teachers and students.

Individual or Small-Group Hardware

These handy devices have multiple uses in all content areas. They are usually less expensive than the larger-ticket whole-class hardware systems. They can also act to elevate the instructional delivery techniques and learning outcomes for both teachers and students.

Microphones and Speakers

Schools may be interested in installing and using audio amplification systems. These require behind-the-scenes wiring and function like a sound system in an auditorium. There is a central unit that connects to a wireless microphone, and when the microphone is spoken into, the sound emits from speakers. Speakers are placed at strategic locations around the room so that anything spoken into the microphone is amplified equally to all corners. Audio amplification is less about volume and more about clarity, although the use of such a system means that the teacher can talk in a normal voice and not strain him- or herself trying to be heard by those at the back of the classroom. In a whitepaper published by LightSPEED Technologies, author Christie Blazer (2008) explains the benefits of using audio systems with students. These systems minimize distractions and tune students in to the teacher's voice, elevating their attention to the content. This leads to more time on task and less repetition of instruction for greater classroom productivity. Moreover, students can use a handheld microphone to read, respond, and report in the classroom, making them feel like classroom rock stars.

Classrooms without the benefit of an audio amplification system can still take advantage of this type of technology. Teachers might pool resources to invest in a portable sound system, much like a mini–PA (public address) system. Small systems, suitable for most teachers, require little power and, therefore, cost less money. Because most teachers cannot project their voices directly above every student, sound will lose momentum by the time it reaches the back of the classroom. However, even small systems can boost sound enough to increase student attention by minimizing background noises. Also, some systems may come with only a wired microphone, which can limit student participation options, necessitating the student to come to the front of the room to read, share, and report on the topic at hand.

Another option for teachers wanting to use a classroom amplification system is to invest in a USB (universal serial bus) wireless microphone. This device works similarly to a wireless mouse. Teachers simply insert the USB device into a computer and use a wireless microphone in their classrooms. The sound is projected through the computer's speakers.

Classroom amplification systems aside, teachers can use classroom computer microphones and speakers for many instructional benefits. In Chapter 3, the idea of young students recording themselves reading was mentioned. Subsequently, the teacher could access, assess, and reflect on the student's audio (using a running record), keeping a record to share with parents or guardians as needed. Moreover, students can add recorded audio to slide show presentations and other digital projects. In Chapter 5, the use of Voki for classroom presentations was introduced. This online program allows students to record any number of short presentations. When they go to share their summary, idea, or report, their avatar speaks for them. This particular strategy might be especially useful for students who are painfully shy, need to build confidence, and/or who struggle with speech and language. Voki offers lesson ideas on its website, such as reciting a poem, practicing a foreign language, recording vocabulary sentences, or explaining how to solve a particular math problem.

Finally, teachers and students can use their computer's microphone and speaker system for video chatting with professionals, field experts, classrooms around the world, or classrooms down the hall. They might use a digital video camera to create a dynamic presentation, and then download it and play it on a classroom computer. The teacher or students might join a webinar or create one that allows for interactive participation on behalf of the group, using the computer's microphone and speaker system to listen to and participate in the webinar.

Wireless Mice and Keyboards

Wireless remotes are inexpensive. For classrooms with just one teacher station and a projector, these little gems put interactive learning right into the palms of students' hands. For example, a teacher may bring up an interactive math game to reinforce the addition and subtraction of fractions. Rather than the teacher running the game from the one computer and calling on students here and there to answer the computation questions, students can click and drag their way through the game themselves when given access to a wireless remote. Wireless mice work with a USB port. The USB device is placed in the computer and connects wirelessly with the mouse, up to a certain distance. In addition to the distance restriction, the other disadvantage is that it is battery operated, occasionally requiring replacements.

Susan Dymoke's (2008) provisional findings suggest that using wireless mice and keyboards have *the potential, particularly when used as a motivational tool, to develop pupils' creative engagement with composition processes during small group collaborative writing* (62).

In an even greater technological advancement, wireless mice now come with their very own attached keyboard. Teachers may find the perfect online game or simulation requiring typing or tapping of keyboard keys. So even though students may be engaged with the clicking and dragging, the teacher needs to run back and forth to the computer, or stay behind the desk, away from the students. A wireless mouse with a keyboard attachment alleviates this. It is an all-in-one device that also works through the USB port. Students can click and drag using the mouse and type using the attached wireless keyboard. (While a wireless keyboard separate from the mouse is always an option, this would take up two USB drives, and students would have two things to pass around to each other.)

Photo Capturing and Video Recording Devices

In the past, when someone wanted to take a picture, he or she would pull out his or her stand-alone digital camera. The same was true for video recording. Today, most digital cameras are equipped to take video footage. Smartphones, too, come with both cameras and video recording capabilities. This makes their ease of use even more accessible for teachers and students. Gayle Berthiaume (2013) has published a list of "100 Ways to Use Digital Cameras" in the classroom. Topping the list are recording images and video on field trips (or simple trips around the school or school grounds), using photos to demonstrate vocabulary words, and documenting a plant's growth from the moment it germinates. As an example of this last idea, teachers can take still-frames of their plants and put the photos together in a movie-making program to see a time-lapse video of their plants' growth. These easy-to-implement ideas support all aspects of learning and provide a record of events and processes from the students' perspectives.

Other recording devices include *flip cams*, or pocket video cameras. Users simply point the camera and press a button to begin recording. Then they attach the device to a computer with the camera's very own attached USB drive. This USB drive "flips" open when it is needed and tucks away when it is not. Because flip cams are so easy to use and provide adequate features for everyday classroom use, the ideas suggested for digital cameras and video cameras apply to these pocket video cameras as well.

While this chapter is almost exclusively devoted to hardware devices to support instruction, digital and video cameras are only as useful as their software. Movie-making software was mentioned earlier in this section as a necessity for putting still photos into motion. Pocket cameras tend to come with their own unique software. Once the device is plugged into the computer, the software automatically loads, and the user may begin creating and editing a movie. Other software programs, such as Movie

Maker, support any digital camera or video camera. Teachers can also access web-based video editing programs, such as JayCut and Animoto. Photo Story is a free download for Windows-based computers that runs from the computer, not the Internet.

Finally, teachers should know a little about the format of the pictures and movies they make. For example, every time someone saves a document in Microsoft Word, it saves as a .docx file. This is the format of the document. Only people who have Microsoft Word or a program that converts the document to a file readable on their own computer can open the file. The same is true of picture files and movie files. Apple users likely save video as .m4v files, while Windows users save video as .mp4 files. There are a lot of image file formats, such as .jpg, .bmp, .png, and .gif. Each format addresses the document's needs. For example, photos need clearer, complete viewing, whereas illustrations may not need to show so much detail. This affects the size of the file and its clarity when displayed in different image-viewing programs.

Webcams

A hardware device closely related to digital cameras and video cameras is the *webcam*. This device comes standard on most computers and laptops. It is a small video recording camera embedded in the computer or laptop. Webcams make video chatting as easy as logging into an email account. (Note: Video chatting as a valuable instructional tool was mentioned in the previous chapter.) Teachers may use webcams (both their own and others') to bring faraway, nebulous topics to the forefront of students' consciousness. Examples include following along with racers in the annual Iditarod, diving to the farthest depths of the ocean with JASON Learning, sharing the birth of zoo animals from a zoo-cam, or sharing others' challenges as they work through the process of surviving a natural disaster. Students can join others' webcam documentaries, and they can create their own. If natural occurrences or current events that directly affect students are worth sharing with the outside world, teachers and students can use their own webcam to record and document their own place in history and post their videos on a student-friendly sharing site for others to view.

A *webcam* is a small video recording camera embedded in the computer or laptop.

eReaders

eReaders and tablets are becoming more and more like small computers, with snap-on keyboards and USB drives; however, they are different from their computer counterparts in some important ways. eReaders are portable and easily carried from one place to the next. They weigh roughly 6 ounces and fit neatly into backpacks, desks, and lockers. They are not tied down to an Ethernet computer station on a tabletop with a chair. Students may curl up anywhere, on the floor, in the library, or in a designated reading area, open their eBooks and start reading. Many eBooks are interactive. In an online article from the *New York Times*, author Thomas J. Fitzgerald (2012) explains, "In *Pete the Cat: I Love My White Shoes*, an eBook for children ages 3 to 7, they can change the color of Pete's shoes by touching them, sing along to music with the lyrics that roll along the page, listen to a narrator, or record their voices as they read aloud" (para. 5). eBooks offer students a level of interaction that hard-copy books will never be able to accomplish.

As advantageous as eReaders are for classroom use, they come with certain challenges. Because of their small size and portability, they can break easily. Yes, they fit easily into backpacks and lockers, but they are handled by children, who may be prone to shoving them unceremoniously between books and burrying them under gym shoes. Aside from being broken, they can also get misplaced, tossed under a bed, or left on the bus. Students will likely be tempted (and even attempt) to download unapproved apps and games or load inappropriate music files. Additionally, eReaders, like tablets, need Internet connectivity through a service provider or access to a school's wireless network. This latter situation will not necessarily allow students to access online resources at home, if they do not have wireless capabilities there.

Teaching students about responsibility and accountability may turn these challenges into life learning experiences for themselves and their belongings. Schools could also restrict the use of the devices, but this would negate the reason to use them. eReaders can house textbooks, online learning games, digital homework files, and much more, so students can extend their classroom learning to their homes. If students can use eReaders only in class, they lose half of the devices' educational benefits. Schools may emphasize personal responsibility by having students and families sign contracts or agreements for use. A designated person at school may regularly collect the devices and "sweep" them for illegal content, providing an opportunity for schools to also download any software updates that may be necessary for optimal operation. Technology specialists at the school and district level or outside agencies should be able to help schools organize and maintain devices for student use.

eReaders have many valuable uses in 21st Century classrooms, many of which mirror the use of tablets or other mobile devices. First and foremost, students can use them to read. They can read a wide variety of narrative (mythology, fables, and realistic fiction) and informational (articles, textbooks, biographies and autobiographies, and maps and other primary source documents) texts. While they read, students can flag and highlight text and look up unknown words. Many library systems and virtual library systems have resources for teachers to use with students, many of them free of charge. Creative Commons licenses have helped with this. These are sets of licenses and contracts that authors and publishers can apply to their work to grant the public free access to stories and texts. Foundations such as the CK–12 Foundation, which sponsors access to textbooks, and Project Gutenberg, which sponsors access to literature, provide sites where students can download free text resources onto their eReaders. Teachers can also find free or inexpensive eBook downloads from publishing companies. Teachers might also try authors' websites and publishers' websites, as mentioned in Chapter 3, for access to free online literature.

eReaders usually come with their own set of apps, most of which are instructionally focused and can be downloaded onto both mobile and stationary hardware. Many apps also allow several registrations on one account, enabling teachers to load them onto several devices without additional costs. eReader apps work great with IWBs, too. Teachers with iPads are not able to connect with an IWB; however, iPad 2 and higher devices can use a VGA (video graphics array) adapter, although the whiteboard's interactive features are nonfunctional. Instead, users need to manipulate objects on the screen of the iPad itself. Teachers can project and demonstrate how to use a particular app, and then students can use eReaders to follow suit, completing a series of tasks as directed by their teacher. For classrooms with multiple eReaders, teachers can follow general organizational patterns, such as small-group guided reading or literature circles, and assign independent reading.

eReaders have benefits for differentiating instruction to meet the needs of special needs and advanced readers. Teachers can match text levels to students' reading abilities and scaffold increasing levels of text complexity using eReader texts just as they can with hard-copy guided reading or leveled texts. Additionally, eReaders provide audio text, allowing students to hear and follow along with stories before attending to reading comprehension tasks independently. Finally, eReader text may be enlarged for students with vision impairments.

Hardware Specific to Instructional Objectives

In addition to the items listed in Chapter 4, teachers may find new interactive digital hardware each school year as they peruse catalogs, read blogs, and join social networks to expand their knowledge of digital learning equipment that is content specific.

> Remember that technology use that is anchored in solid educational objectives is what makes technology a valuable educational tool. Using technology for technology's sake does little good. It must be aligned to specific educational objectives (Grinager 2006).

Here are some examples of and uses for interactive digital hardware:

- GeoSafari has talking microscopes and talking globes. They also have several varieties of digital magniscopes that are handheld microscopes.

- Hot Dots are cards with text or picture directives. Students are directed to find and identify the main idea of a passage or solve multistep math problems. The answer choices have "hot dots." Students use a special pen to indicate their answers. If they are correct, they are rewarded with lights or sounds. If they are incorrect, the pen directs them to make another selection.

- A portable digital weather station may be used as part of students' preparation for a show that broadcasts to the school each morning. Students can take readings of wind direction and wind speed, temperature and humidity, and dew point.

- Electronic hardware can greatly enhance a school's video recording studio. Soundboards, video mixers, and wireless microphones and video recorders can add to an already excellent setup.

- Engineering-minded teachers can use electronic "toys" to teach science concepts such as electricity, force, and motion. Interlocking block companies make construction sets that also come with available motors and operational equipment. Even young students can apply their creative talents to building a robotic device and engineer a system that uses technology to operate it.

Conclusion

Typically when teachers think of technology, they think of their computers and the Internet. Certainly, these two items are essential staples for 21st Century classrooms. Other technology hardware, although not as readily used, is equally valuable as part of a teacher's toolkit. Digital equipment suits whole-class instruction, targets small-group or individual students or computer use, and expands the interest level and value of learning through content-specific hardware options. Whether teachers have one computer or several, whether they are working at a one-to-one school or not, these hardware options will help them expand their digital classrooms and redefine teaching and learning for both themselves and their students.

Reflect and Respond

1. Of the hardware options described in this chapter, which do you have access to and want to use more regularly? Alternatively, which would you most like to have access to?

2. How do you see the use of this hardware improving the overall academic achievement of your students? What instructional objectives can this hardware help your students meet?

3. How can the use of this hardware enhance how you integrate technology in the classroom?

4. Would this hardware be better suited for use with the whole class, in small groups, or with individual students? Think of an alternate use where you encompass it for a different organization of students or for a different purpose.

Chapter 7

Assistive Technology for Special-Needs Students

As teachers, we know that there is no one-size-fits-all approach to educating children. They have varied needs, from those who require one-on-one assistance for daily life skills, such as eating and communicating, to those who excel beyond standard curriculum and require meaningful, relevant challenging projects and assignments at the highest comprehension levels of evaluating and creating. Technology can help with these two exceptional needs and with every other. This chapter explores assistive technology tools that help special needs students and those with unique learning challenges, such as English language learners and gifted students.

According to the Schwab Foundation for Learning (2000), assistive technology tools are items, equipment, or systems that "work around or compensate for learning difficulties" (4). Such tools "can often help teachers personalize lessons and skills enhancement to each child" (Zorigian and Job 2010, para. 1). Where there is a need, there is technology to assist with this need. Today, schools may locate and access more than adequate technology tools that assist students with reading, writing, listening, speaking, math, and social skills. This chapter is divided into three sections:

- assistive technology for students with communication needs (expressive, receptive, or both)

- technology to support English language learners

- technology for students with instructional needs

Of course, there are overlaps in technology among these three ideas. For example, if a student struggles to communicate effectively, he or she also likely requires assistance to read and write. In addition, the age of the students comes into play. Special-needs students in kindergarten may have different communication challenges than fifth grade special-needs students. Consider the value of the technology presented here as it pertains to your students' ages and abilities. Perhaps you do not service students with profound communication needs, but the technology discussed here may benefit your students in other ways.

Technology to Support Expressive and Receptive Language Skills

One widely used tool that students with communication challenges can use is word-processing software. This easily accessible and versatile tool enables students who struggle to speak to share their thoughts and ideas more easily through written text. Likewise, for some students the physical act of writing interferes with their ability to effectively demonstrate their command of written language, especially spelling, punctuation, and grammar. In their study, Orit E. Hetzroni and Betty Shrieber (2004) summarize the benefits of using word processing to enhance classroom academic outcomes with middle-school students in reading, spelling, and overall quality of organization and structure of compositions.

> Through the use of the word processor, all participants reduced spelling errors by using the spell checker feature of the word processor and by keeping spaces between letters and words. The use of the red underline feature of the word processor and the availability of the spell checker increased their awareness of the existence of their errors in the text. (Hetzroni and Shrieber 2004, 152)

With texting, social networking, and email as avenues to interact with others through text, both complex and simple word processing can provide a means of sharing written language for students with speech or writing disabilities.

Alternative Keyboards

For students who lack the skills required for typing, teachers may acquire alternative keyboards. These are helpful for students who struggle to interact effectively with traditional key placements, who need larger key pads, or for students who can type with only one finger or one hand (Lindberg, Flasch Ziegler, and Barczyk 2009). These keyboards are programmable with special overlays to indicate the new key placements. They move the most frequently used keys to new locations, minimizing movement to type words using the most common letters (see Figure 7.1). This may help students by reducing key choices. Keys may be grouped by color, and some overlays include graphics to help with understanding of the keystrokes. Many layouts are available, including QWERTY, Dvorak, Colemak, and Maltron. Keyboards also come with larger keys, increasing the accuracy of keystrokes. On-screen keyboards allow users to type using their mouse—simply point and click. These keyboards also work with a touch screen or alternative mouse, such as a joystick or electronic pointer. Students with limited mobility may benefit from this kind of typing mechanism.

Figure 7.1 Example of an Alternative Keyboard for Right-Handed Typists

Special devices enhance learning opportunities for students who are visually impaired, including

- **Screen enlargers.** These serve as magnifiers for computer screens.

- **Screen readers.** These "read" everything on the screen, from text to graphics to control options.

- **Braille displays.** These special keyboards convert on-screen text into Braille text. As each line of Braille is read, the system can be refreshed to read the next line.

A technology option related to alternative keyboards is the use of a *keyboard filter* or an *abbreviation expander*. This software works with a typist's word-processing program. Instead of the user having to type an entire word, the program uses saved and stored abbreviations to predict and type the most frequently used words with just a few keystrokes. This minimizes the number of keystrokes a student needs to make in order to type fluently. For example, instead of having to type out the entire word *beautiful*, a student may just need to begin typing *b-e-a* and the whole word will pop up.

The following alternative input devices respond to user input just as a standard keyboard and mouse do, but through varied techniques.

- Alternative keyboards change the size, color, and placement of the keys.

- Electronic pointers allow computer users to control the cursor without the use of hands.

- Interactive whiteboards (IWBs) provide a larger response area so that students with physical limitations can more easily indicate their responses and choices with regard to software and online programs.

- Joysticks may be used with the hands, feet, teeth, and/or chin to control the cursor on the screen.

- Tangible pointers, usually worn on the head or held with teeth, allow computer users to type without the use of hands.

- Touch screens do not require the use of a mouse. All the options and features may be selected by touching them on the screen, or using pointers or joysticks, as mentioned previously.

- Trackballs control the cursor easily with a simple spin (versus having to hold and move an entire mouse).

Speech-to-Text Tools

Closely related to word processing are speech-to-text tools. These programs support both speaking and writing skill challenges. Students who struggle to write but have adequate speaking abilities may use a speech-to-text program to dictate their ideas. The computer and program use voice recognition to convert the spoken words into text on the screen. Early research indicates that this assistive tool "helps students with [learning disabilities] and other struggling writers compensate for problems with basic transcription" (MacArthur, Graham, and Fitzgerald 2006, 255). This voice recognition software can also allow computer users to speak commands rather than use a mouse or keyboard to accomplish related tasks, such as changing fonts, opening new documents, adding images, and composing email messages to specific recipients. Students who struggle to speak can type what they want to say, and then have the computer recite the text orally. This program gives voice to those who otherwise may have none or who are limited in their speaking skills. Both speech-to-text and text-to-speech programs are beneficial to the visually impaired who need to use a computer to communicate with others in writing.

> For students with hearing difficulties, technology tools such as light signal alerts and personal FM listening systems can keep them more actively involved in the general classroom happenings.

Portable Communicators

Portable communicators are durable devices that provide everyday talk with the push of a button. These devices may be programmed with a limited number of messages, such as "I am hungry" and "I need to go to the bathroom." Using visual cues, children may press the appropriate button at the appropriate moment, providing their teachers with important information in real time. Also, these devices may be programmed with everyday conversation starters, such as "What did you do this weekend?" and "Do you want to play kickball with me?" These messages help support students who lack adequate social interaction skills and need more concrete direction interacting with other students. Moreover, portable communicators can support students' literacy skills. Teachers may record stories or comprehension questions. Students may use the devices to listen to stories as they follow along in reading books and can practice independent learning skills by listening to and completing tasks that have been recorded specifically for them.

One app is SoundingBoard, which converts Apple products into portable communicators that include preloaded options as well as personally created boards with symbols or pictures to accommodate specific needs. For example, teachers and students can program boards with conversational messages for the lunchroom. One preloaded board includes common expressions, so students can express themselves at a moment's notice appropriately.

Technology for English Language Learners

Technology tools and devices not only enhance learning opportunities for students with disabilities, but they also can help students learn English. In an article written for the New York State United Teachers (NYSUT) publication, *Educator's Voice*, authors Elizabeth Brozek and Debra Duckworth summarize, "English language learners in particular benefit from the reinforcement of vocabulary and concepts through pictures, graphics and video. They also benefit from being able to use technology to express themselves. Technology helps English language learners find a voice, easing the transition to a new language" (2011, 15). Digital translators, English-learning software, and interactive reading and language games can provide substantial support for students whose first language is not English. With so many electronic devices and resources to choose from, teachers may get caught up in technology for technology's sake and forget the mainstay of their lessons: instructional objectives.

Michael Morgan (2008) cautions teachers to not overload students with too much digital power. He offers a three-step process for determining what technology to use.

1. Investigate the programs and resources to be sure they are suitable for classroom use and appropriate to the students' English learning levels.

2. Identify how this technology benefits English language learners.

3. Create English language learning objectives, and use the technology as a means to an end, not an end in itself.

Text-to-speech technology is of particular benefit to ELLs since they can use it to gain individual support in their studies and to learn proper English pronunciations of English words and phrases (Kurzweil Educational Systems 2004).

Electronic Translators

Electronic translators allow anyone who speaks any language to have words and phrases translated from English into his or her native language and vice versa. Franklin is one company that has been manufacturing speaking dictionaries and similar devices for many years. Various products are available that provide a full-color screen and visual dictionary to help students. Translators are also available as downloadable apps for personal devices. Most are free, and they offer translations for several languages. These are helpful if students have personal smartphones or tablets that they can use and carry with them during the school day. Teachers (and schools) can order translation software for use on classroom computers or in lab settings. These software programs can include a text-to-speech feature, requiring the use of a headset with a microphone. Finally, online translators can support students with written and spoken language using any device that has access to the Internet. These programs usually are not quite as accurate as software written specifically for translation. As with any translation program, software, or device, teachers and students should take care to ensure the messages they want to get across are the intended ones.

Electronic Dictionaries

Along the lines of online translators are electronic dictionaries. Students can access any number of references online or through personal devices to hear words spoken in English, used in complete sentences, defined, and related to other words. Translation dictionaries intended for younger students often include pictures and interactive, cartoonlike features. Although these may seem "babyish" for older students, these students may benefit from the visual and audio support provided. These interactive programs are useful for both teachers and students, as they may both have expressive and receptive language translated into understandable language. For example, a teacher can translate directions into the student's primary language. Likewise, a student can have his or her message translated from the primary language into English so that the teacher understands the message. Translation dictionaries are also available as stand-alone devices, similar to the electronic translators previously described. These dictionaries allow the user to see and hear isolated words in both languages, used in context. Students may also access synonyms and antonyms, and hear the words spoken aloud.

Teachers of English language learners (ELLs) can use IWBs and interactive games and activities to engage students in meaningful language learning while they hone and practice their listening and speaking skills. The use of IWBs offer opportunities for students to participate actively in learning (Brozek and Duckworth 2011).

Digital Learning Media

Digital learning media in particular is very useful because teachers have access to thousands of illustrations, images, photos, and videos to "show" the words as they are explained, helping build needed vocabulary skills (Brozek and Duckworth 2011). The ideas for the use of interactivity with ELLs are limitless. Teachers can create (or find) interactive games and activities for pretty much any reading or language skill to use with an IWB, including playing matching word games and fill-in-the-blank games, highlighting text, completing graphic organizers, and editing. These types of activities also lend themselves to the total physical response (TPR) method of teaching and learning for ELLs. TPR was developed in the 1960s by American psychology professor James Asher (Bowen 2013). With this method, students respond to commands using physical movements in lieu of verbal responses. For example, students may point to words or pictures to answer a question, or they may perform simple movements to demonstrate their thinking (e.g., "Stand up if you agree that we see the sun during the daytime"). Since students physically move objects, words, pictures, or other stimuli on the interactive whiteboard to practice a skill, they are engaged in TPR.

Movies and online videos are helpful tools for all learners, as previously discussed in Chapters 3 and 5. Students just learning English may especially benefit from increased opportunities to view and learn from any program or file where visual images accompany audio. Video usage includes watching informative clips on content, processes, procedures, vocabulary usage, or skills. Teachers can create their own video clips (or borrow some from other teachers) to explain and demonstrate a process, and then encourage their students to access them. This can be used before learning as a previewing strategy, during learning as a practice strategy, and after learning as a review strategy. Since these videos may be accessed at any time, students may return to them as needed throughout their coursework.

Along with using video that includes audio and visual instructional support, eReaders, audiobooks, MP3 downloads, podcasts, and digital texts can benefit English language learners as much as general education students. Any time teachers can add audio or video to a student's instructional day and provide repeated exposure to language over time, the student stands a greater chance of assimilating this information into permanent memory. This is partly because about 65 percent of the population are visual learners (Mind Tools 2014, under "Visual Learners"). These students learn best when their teachers use visuals such as pictures and images, and videos to teach concepts and skills (Hutton 2013). Additionally, auditory learners, which make up about 30 percent of the population (Mind Tools, under "Auditory Learners"), benefit from information presented verbally (Farwell 2012, under "Visual, Auditory, Kinesthetic Learners").

Technology can also allow students to access the English text in their native language. Providing first language support while students learn English can help students attend to comprehension without the stress of having to read only English, which may include many unfamiliar words, phrases, and idiomatic expressions that take time to learn and understand.

At any time during instruction when students come up against words with which they are unfamiliar, an instant online search may show pictures, images, or diagrams to illustrate and better explain concepts for students. It takes only a moment to conduct a quick search online—about the same amount of time, as the teacher would need to explain the term or concept in depth. Even then, teachers may end up scratching out a quick drawing on a whiteboard or paper to further student understanding.

In this digital age, what do adults do if they want to learn a new language? Although some may seek out and join a foreign language class, many turn to the Internet or a language learning program, such as Rosetta Stone. As much as this and related software programs benefit English speakers wanting to learn a different language, they also may benefit ELLs as they begin to learn English. While general education students may access instructional support programs that differentiate learning unique to them and their needs, ELLs may use a language-learning program to build their understanding of English listening and speaking skills. There are many software programs to choose from. Some require the use of a headset (or speakers) with a microphone (or embedded microphone). Teachers should be aware of the hardware requirements to successfully run a program such as this, as well as what the software has to offer.

Tools for Supporting Reading and Listening Comprehension

- **Smart pens.** These pens write and record lectures and digitize written words, syncing them to review at a later time. Also, the information can be uploaded to a computer for full access from anywhere.

- **Reading pens.** Users scan text and then hear it spoken aloud. This handy device may be used with just about any printed text. Some will scan and send text to a computer where it may be highlighted, bolded, underlined, or changed with any word-processing function.

Technology to Support Instruction

In an article published in *The Future of Children*, authors Ted S. Hasselbring and Candyce H. Williams Glaser (2000) remind us, "Not only can computer technology facilitate a broader range of educational activities to meet a variety of needs for students with mild learning disorders, but adaptive technology now exists than can enable even those students with severe disabilities to become active learners in the classroom alongside their peers who do not have disabilities" (102). In this chapter, we have already explored how technology can meet the requirements of special needs students. Now let us look at technology to support academics, beyond what has already been addressed.

Outlining and Graphic Organizers

Beyond the obvious instructional computer and online programs that assess students' skill needs and target instruction through modules and activities specific to them, software programs can ease lesson planning and support students in their academic endeavors. First, outlining and concept-mapping software, such as Kidspiration and Inspiration, allow students to conceptualize ideas and make sense of what may seem like disconnected concepts. These two particular products are also available as apps, extending their usefulness since they may be used on any personal device. Students can create their own outlines or maps, or teachers can create them for students, allowing them to add details and information naturally throughout a course of study. The advantage of having students create their own visual representations is that they can process information into a synthesized abbreviated summary. The advantage to having the teacher create the representations is that it saves class time, minimizes the output students must attend to, and keeps the instructional focus on a clear path.

Graphic organizers are common, useful instructional support tools. As they listen to, read, or otherwise acquire information, students may organize the content into any appropriate structure, such as cause and effect, main idea and details, or sequence of events. Many graphic organizers are available free online. Also, teachers may use a "smart" feature embedded within the program to insert and modify a graphic organizer using one of the templates. The advantage to using digital versions of graphic organizers is that teachers can save them electronically and reprint them later. Additionally, they can be emailed to students, posted to a class website, or stored in the cloud where students may access them anytime. Once students become accustomed to their teacher's expectations for completing the organizers, students access particular ones for particular purposes to work on independently. For students who need additional support, teachers can add more specific directions or sentence starters, or they can partially complete the information for students, limiting the amount of information students need to add. For example, a teacher may provide the main ideas of a reading selection and have students include only the details that support them, or vice versa. Teachers may include the terms and definitions or descriptions in a three-column chart, and require students to add only the examples or illustrations. This effectively scaffolds the task for students. As a result, they need not expend all of their energy looking for all of the information—just the information the teacher decides he or she wants them to focus on.

The use of outlining and mapping software and graphic organizers helps students receive, organize, hold, and retrieve information they must know to become literate students not only in language arts, but also in their content-area studies. These are the modern-day versions of note-taking. What was once a painstaking process for students at the elementary, middle, high school, and even college levels has become an efficient task thanks to note-taking software and apps. Whether students use programs specifically designed for note-taking, sticky-note software, or word-processing programs, they can organize information quickly and meaningfully, and always have ready access to their thinking and recording. The benefit of any of these programs is that students can identify the most important topics or information by reorganizing it in the outline, stacking virtual sticky notes in a meaningful order, or using text features, such as highlighting or underlining text, to easily identify the main points. These types of programs also enable students to make note of essential vocabulary terms. When such a note-taking program is paired with a vocabulary-building learning program, students can refer to their notes and reference essential terms quickly and efficiently on their computers or personal devices.

Text-to-speech functions, highlighted earlier in the chapter, need not be reserved only for communicating reading material. Talking calculators allow students to hear the numbers, symbols, or operations being entered, and they will verbalize the answers to the problems. For students who struggle with numeration or computation skills, these devices may provide the necessary support for them to more accurately record the math problems and answers that they intend.

Conclusion

Technology provides ready access to content and information for all students. In particular, specialized hardware and software can benefit students with special needs, whether those needs are cognitive, social, physical, behavioral, or in any combination. Devices that aid in computer function facilitate communication and support instructional delivery in the classroom at the student's level. They can assist special needs students to successfully contribute to class discussions and interact with their peers. Hardware and software also support ELLs with devices and programs to help develop English language skills, including reading, writing, speaking, and listening. Where there is a need, someone develops a piece of technology to fulfill it. Students with special needs are no exception to the technological benefits that schools can offer students.

Reflect and Respond

1. How can the technology you already have available support students with special needs and ELLs?

2. How might technology support how you assess the academic progress of your students?

3. Think about a time when you needed to differentiate instruction or support a student or students (by extending learning or supporting learning). How did you use technology to provide differentiated instruction?

4. What new strategy, technique, or technology might you try the next time you are faced with a need to differentiate instruction for special needs students or English language learners?

Chapter 8

Assessment in the Digital Age

Testing and assessment have evolved over the past few decades. How to test, when to test, and why to test dominate many conversations at schools and in school districts, leaving some educators feeling as if they spend more time testing than teaching. At the same time, the practice of testing itself has not changed in fifty years. Teachers teach, students learn, students take tests, and teachers evaluate student learning based on test results. According to Bill Tucker (2009), "With technology changing at a rapid pace, we have many of the tools to create vastly improved assessment systems and practices" (52). The advent of word-processing programs allows teachers to design and create their own tests with ease. Test-taking hardware and software, as mentioned in Chapter 2, allow students to digitally submit their answer choices and receive instant feedback regarding their selections. Additionally, Tucker acknowledges that "technologies, which feature the efficiency and consistency of machine-read scoring along with cognitively challenging, open-ended performance tasks, can help [educators] build assessments that move beyond bubble-filling and, at the same time, offer rigorous and reliable evidence of student learning" (48).

This chapter explores these testing options and more. It also discusses challenges that educators face with technology-based testing and how they might overcome these challenges.

Formative Assessments

Teachers use *formative assessments* to inform instruction. Larry Ainsworth (2007) defines *common* formative assessments as "assessments *for* learning that are collaboratively designed, administered, scored, and analyzed by team members" (81). Ainsworth acknowledges teachers' reference to *classroom* formative assessments as "pretests" or "pre-assessments" (84). These assessments are usually informal, quick, and easily scored, but do not count toward a student's grade. For example, a popular classroom formative assessment is the *exit ticket*. Before students leave the classroom or move to another subject, they turn in a completed "ticket" answering a question, providing a solution to a problem, or responding to what they have learned. Exit tickets enable teachers to quickly check the status of the class (what was learned, what misconceptions exist, what needs more practice) and plan for the next lesson.

Technology facilitates the teacher's use of classroom formative assessments by providing immediate feedback. As with the exit ticket, the teacher can have students respond to questions via a social networking account or through email. Students who do not have access to either of these may still write their responses on paper.

One benefit to having students post their responses online is that students can also ask questions that the teacher can incorporate into the next day's lesson. Alternatively, the teacher may choose to respond immediately to the student's question, minimizing the time between the student's question and an answer.

Teachers having students reflect on their own learning using self-evaluation rating scales (as described previously) can make the system more formal by asking students to encode their rating into a student response system. In this scenario, the teacher has the question recorded in the program's software. Students use a handheld device to log their response. The advantage of this system is that the teacher (and students) can immediately see where the class is along the continuum of learning using the system's instant graphing display. As concepts are reintroduced and reviewed, the same question with the same scale may be posed to students. This data, when added to the previous data, will show the class's progress overall with a particular skill.

Student response systems need not be purchased separately. "Bring-your-own-device" or "bring-your-own-technology" schools and one-to-one schools can turn any personal computer, tablet, or smartphone into a student response device using a program called Socrative. The applications available with this program work similarly to formal response systems, except teachers use their Socrative account to upload quizzes, and students log into their teacher's account and use their personal devices to respond to the test items.

Teachers can use student response systems as quick checks of student learning. For example, teachers can post just three to five simple math computation or word problems for students to solve. They can post the same number of language arts questions related to multiple-meaning words or contractions. They can ask vocabulary-related questions using science or social studies content words. In just a few moments, teachers will immediately know, in real time, how the class is faring with regard to current instructional objectives.

Teachers can use apps for formative assessment as well. The Bubble Sheet app from MasteryConnect allows teachers to have students complete a digital bubble sheet. This works similarly to the student response system, except students bubble in their answers instead of using a handheld device. This is an option for schools without student response systems. Another app, Random Name Selector Lite by Walsall Academy, allows teachers to randomly select students to respond to questions or explain processes. Both apps are available through iTunes.

Many teachers like to give their students informal surveys or inventories (e.g., to get to know his or her students or for parents to provide feedback about important classroom routines and concerns). Today, teachers are equipped to post surveys (many are free) that they create using online survey software and have students and/or parents respond digitally. The data is captured and reported quantitatively and in chart form for easy and quick analysis. Teachers can also use online survey programs for students to explain what they already know about a topic before the class delves into it too deeply. This valuable informal feedback is useful as teachers design and plan instruction based on students' prior knowledge and experience with selected topics.

Using Technology for Assessment: Benefits for Teachers and Students

- **Instant feedback.** Teachers learn who "gets it." Students learn how and where they made their mistakes without having to wait for the teacher to pass back tests.

- **Ease of scoring and grading.** Teachers no longer need to spend hours checking papers. Results can be organized in an electronic system for easy analysis. Students gauge where they are along the learning path toward the instructional outcome.

- **Opportunity for interactive assessment items.** Teachers who use interactive technology to teach concepts and skills know the assessments they give students better match their instruction. Students can "see" problems come alive on screen, providing an added level of support.

- **Less instructional time lost.** Teachers can continue with lessons as soon as students finish an electronic assessment. Teachers can re-use electronic assessments from year to year. Students do not have to wait for everyone to finish the test before they can get back to learning.

- **Reduced chances of cheating.** Teachers can employ software and settings to minimize students' opportunities to cheat. Students know their results are an honest reflection of their learning.

Summative Assessments

Summative assessments generally come after instruction. Teachers use these tests to determine whether students "got it" and to what extent. These tests, that everyone takes, are given to determine which students have mastered the class, course content, or state curriculum. Jay McTighe and Ken O'Connor (2005) list familiar summative assessments as tests, performance tasks, final exams, culminating projects, and work portfolios.

They add, "Evaluative assessments command the attention of students and parents because their results typically "count" and appear on report cards and transcripts." These tests might have multiple-choice responses to ease the daunting task of grading or scoring them. They might also include short or extended written responses, or gridded responses. Students might record their answers on an answer sheet that is scanned and scored by a computer.

While paper-and-pencil summative assessments are still used, they are being quickly replaced by electronic versions. Online testing in education is growing in popularity. These assessments allow for interactive features, such as text-to-speech and highlighting. They are also capable of breathing life into assessment items with animation and manipulative icons. For example, to solve a math word problem on a paper-and-pencil math assessment, students read the problem on the page, and then use a workspace or scratch paper to work it out. Traditional test answers would be either recorded on an answer line or marked on the bubbles of a scan sheet. This same math problem online might include a simple animation to illustrate what is happening. Students can use interactive features, such as typing, click and drag, and embedded computerized calculators or rulers, to work on the problem. Students might still choose an A, B, or C answer, but all of their work may be captured and stored digitally. Online tests can also be started and stopped (and saved) as needed to meet students' schedules. Students no longer must sit knee to back in a confined space for hours, waiting for others to finish. Once they complete the test, students may simply exit the system. If school schedules only allow for one-hour testing sessions, testing administrators can more easily accommodate a two-hour test when the test is administered electronically. No more sitting, listening to ten minutes of directions, passing out booklets, checking booklets, and re-collecting booklets. The computer can accomplish all of this in a shorter amount of time, and teachers become monitors to ensure test validity and compliance with testing rules. Electronically submitted answers provide faster results back to students and schools as well. Some online tests even offer immediate results following the final submission. No more waiting and wondering about scores.

Just as student response systems may be used for formative assessments and quick checks of student learning, they may also be used for summative assessments. The disadvantage to this is that students who take a long time to complete one test item hold up everyone in the same testing session since only one question may be displayed at a time. For this reason, teachers may still distribute and re-collect tests, requiring students to record their answers on another sheet of paper. These same tests may be used in subsequent school years or with other classes. Once a test has been entered into the response system software program, students may simply use the response device to enter their answer choices. Teachers may still benefit from having their tests scored electronically, saving valuable time both in and out of school.

Another option is for teachers to use an online quiz-making tool. QuizStar is a web-based quiz maker where teachers can create and students can take quizzes online. Since this is an electronic system, all quizzes are scored automatically, and teachers can access results after everyone has finished the test. This program provides many options for teachers with regard to test questions, including linking multimedia files, adding short-response items, and using settings to maximize or restrict immediate feedback.

Immediate feedback has been mentioned several times as an advantage with regard to both formative and summative assessments. Robert J. Marzano, Debra Pickering, and Jane E. Pollock (2001) identified timely feedback as one highly effective instructional technique that teachers should utilize in their classrooms. *Feedback given immediately after a test-like situation is best. In general, the more delay that occurs in giving feedback, the less improvement there is in achievement* (97).

Chapter 5 explored the idea of interactive graphing using online websites. As part of today's testing environment, students might use a similar graphing function either to demonstrate how to graph a certain situation or to analyze and adjust a graph based on information from the problem. Chapter 5 also covered using online simulations to help students visualize and critically contemplate science-related ideas. Similar simulation tasks might appear in online testing settings. So, instead of students reading a science question and choosing or guessing an answer based on knowledge they may or may not have, students can complete an online simulation to demonstrate the steps in a process or manipulate variables to reach a particular outcome.

An article published by *U.S. News and World Report* (Clark 2008) explained how college professors are using anti-plagiarism software and anti-cheating software to maintain more honest learning and testing atmospheres. Anti-plagiarism software compares students' work to databases which house millions of texts written by students, web sites, and publishing companies. Once analyzed, the professor may decide how similar is too similar, and determine the extent to which a student plagiarized. Some test centers are using fingerprint and palm scans to ensure that the person who shows up to take a college level test is actually the person assigned to do so. Test centers might have video-monitored desks with cheat-proof computers where students sit and take their tests. Once popularized, high schools might consider these technology advances as well to enhance their own programs.

Shifting to Electronic Testing

Schools that have successfully shifted to electronic testing have done so over several years. Knowing that state and national summative assessments are or will be moving to online formats, district technology coordinators have had time to process the idea and devise a plan for their schools so that both students and teachers are ready for it. One huge benefit of all this hype, according to Dian Schaffhauser (2013), is that schools and districts that have been actively preparing for online summative assessments "will presumably be better outfitted for digitally supported instructional practices" (6). Since some schools, districts, and states are further along in this preparation process, those that follow can discover and learn from those that are ready. In some districts, this has led to an upgrade of online and server connections, rather than hardware operating systems. In others, this has meant budgeting to increase quantities of newer computers or devices to accommodate the quantity of students needing to test within a certain time frame.

Advantages and Disadvantages to Online Assessment

Textbook companies are now providing online testing options for teachers, which offers several advantages. First and foremost, these assessments have the potential to save thousands of dollars in paper costs. Online testing means no printing. No sorting, no stapling, and no handing out of papers; no re-collection of stacks of papers; and no need to stuff those papers into a satchel or carryall bag and lug them home to grade, only to lug them back to school again to redistribute to students. Students simply sit at a computer, pull up their tests (likely assigned by the teacher in the textbook's online system), take the test, and save or submit their answers. The computer system scores all the students' tests. Teachers then access the online report to see how students fared. Some programs will allow exports of scores into a spreadsheet program. The teacher can then import the scores into a gradebook program. With just a few keystrokes, an entire class or multiple classes of tests are scored, and the grading process is completed.

Of course, all of this sounds wonderful. However, online testing comes with challenges, too. Logistical and funding issues must first be addressed before students can access their online tests. Schools need an adequate number of computers and the infrastructure to support these computers being online at the same time. Also, teachers must factor in the time it takes students to access the online system, take the test, and log out. Teachers without the benefit of one-to-one technology must sign up for a lab, whether it is stationary or portable. Ever mindful of the time, they must also have a plan in case something goes awry; students do not finish or are absent. Many of these obstacles can be overcome with a little creative thinking and forward planning. Teachers may provide a paper test and have students simply go the computer to record their answers to the questions. This takes only a minute, and the teacher still saves time from not having to grade each test. If the tests are re-collected, and not written on, the teacher can store them and save them for the following school year, limiting printing costs. Alternatively, the teacher can use a document camera (or a computer and projector, if the test questions are entered into a slide show program) to project the questions. Students can record their answers at their desks for input into the computer later. This latter idea also works for teachers who have access to a student response system. Although better for administering formative assessments, these devices provide the same capabilities as online tests, just through a modified process.

Project-Based Assessments

Using Technology for Project-Based Assessment: Benefits for Teachers and Students

- **Require students to be creative,** a 21st century skill. Teachers can offer students varied means of demonstrating understanding, something that can reenergize students. Students can "think outside the box" and show off their learning in a less pedestrian manner.

- **Encourage collaboration,** another 21st century skill. Teachers can assign group projects to support student learning. Students have the benefit of using each other's talents to create a completed project.

- **Require students to communicate knowledge.** Teachers can determine the formal or informal nature of the project, depending on its purpose. Students can apply various written and oral communication skills to complete it.

- **Promote interdisciplinary concepts and skills.** Teachers can connect content areas to language arts standards. Students can practice essential writing and speaking skills in a less threatening environment (since the focus is on the demonstration of content understanding more so than the delivery of the information).

Project-based assessments (or project-based learning outcomes) are those that students complete to demonstrate knowledge and skills by designing, planning, and producing some instructionally based outcome. In the digital age, project-based assessments usually take the form of a multimedia project. According to Michael Simkins et al. (2002), students' multimedia projects "will be technology-based presentations, such as a computerized slide show, a website, or a video. These presentations will include evidence that… students have mastered key concepts and processes [teachers] need to teach and will be a source of great pride for them and for [the teacher]" (3). As an assessment component, the authors identify three areas to evaluate as part of students' overall assessment:

- activities for developing expectations

- activities for improving the multimedia products

- activities for compiling and disseminating evidence of learning

Any and all of these evaluation measures may be completed using rubrics, rating scales, or checklists. Suggestions for evaluating student projects follow in the next section.

Designing appropriate project-based assessments may pose a challenge. Teachers who use project-based assessments want to know what their students learned, and they want the students to demonstrate their learning through meaningful, creative ways. What does this look like? According to John Larmer and John R. Mergendoller (2010), projects worth spending class time doing are not "meaning-lite." They emphasize that "it is the process of students' learning and the depth of their cognitive engagement—rather than the resulting project—that distinguishes projects from busywork" (34–35). They have identified seven essential components of project-based learning. The first is establishing a clear purpose for completing the project—what they call "need to know." The second is introducing a "driving question," one that will challenge students' thinking about the topic in a unique situation. The third is "student voice and choice." This component gives students options in how they want to complete and present their work. Next is "21st century skills," critical thinking, creativity, communication, and collaboration. The former two ideas will have been established in the first three steps; the latter two will come while students engage in the project. The remaining steps include "inquiry and innovation," "feedback and revision," and "a publicly presented product." The idea here is that meaningful projects go beyond the regurgitation of facts and information, which is a low-level skill that does not require students to think too much. Instead, projects should be original and innovative, requiring students to think, plan, and resolve.

7 Essential Components of Project-Based Learning

1. need to know
2. driving question
3. student voice and choice
4. 21st Century skills
5. inquiry and innovation
6. feedback and revision
7. a publicly presented product

Of course, not all projects lend themselves to this level of inquiry. It is okay for teachers to have students use technology to summarize and explain. However, these types of projects should be distinguished from more meaningful projects. The former let the teacher know that students have learned something. The latter let the teacher know that students can do something with their knowledge. Obviously, learning projects may take many forms.

The following are a few generic examples of using project-based assessment with students.

- Use **Voki** to have students summarize information about a famous or historical person from his or her perspective. Students can also use this resource to record their own vocabulary practices.

- Use a **web-based digital film creation** program to create entertaining interactive summaries about topics or create dialogue between two opposing ideas, such as specific nouns versus strong verbs and their impact on effective essay writing.

- Have students create **interactive, multimedia slide shows** to summarize any number of topics or processes across the content areas. One online resource that might provide a bit more novelty than traditional software is Prezi. This program allows students to shift, zoom, and create a powerful and engaging presentation starting with a blank canvas.

- Use an **infographic creation website** to have students design and create a summary of a text or information, write a persuasive piece, or create an advertisement. An infographic is like a poster. It has simple graphics and text details for easy reading. For example, students might create an infographic comparing different types of angles or explaining why a particular character from a story would make a great friend. Some infographic web resources are easel.ly, Piktochart, and infogr.am.

The following are two specific project-based activities in which teachers had their students participate.

Tectonic Quilt (Art, Geology, Geography, Sociology)

Artist Benjamin Volta worked with fifth graders at Grover Washington, Jr. Middle School in Philadelphia in 2009. Students used their understanding of how communications and technology have changed the world to design and create a 21st century representation of the world today. They drew on their understanding of the slow process of seismic activity to create individual representations of both ideas. Each student's drawing was scanned and assembled along with every other student's drawing to create a comprehensive artistic representation of our world today. With this project, students demonstrated their understanding of tectonic plates from a geological perspective and infused ideas related to technology and its impact on the world both politically and socially to create a "tectonic quilt."

Historical Figure Dialogue (Language Arts, History)

Technology can transform boring and routine into creative and exciting. Online writing programs offer students the opportunity to use interactive tools, which add an element of novelty to their writing. Christopher Kauter from Deer Park, New York, had his tenth grade Deer Park High School history students use Google Story Builder to write and publish a "witty conversation among at least three historical figures" (Wait 2013, para. 1). One student, Christina O'Toole, wrote a humorous dialogue comparing "impressive discoveries" among John Locke, Galileo Galilei, and Archimedes. With this project, students demonstrated their understanding of history and the people who have shaped it into what it is today while applying creative writing skills, including the use of dialogue.

Evaluating Student Work

Project-based learning offers many advantages to students. However, these projects are not easily evaluated by educators and translated into grades, as required by schools and school districts. The best option for evaluating student projects is with a rubric or scale, which may be completed in one of two ways. First, online rubric-building tools, such as Recipes4Success (Tools option), Rubistar, TeAchnology Rubrics, iRubric, and eRubric, allow teachers to quickly create or borrow a rubric that has criteria closely or exactly connected to the teachers' expectations. An example of an online-generated rubric is shown in Figure 8.1. This rubric was created with autocomplete options, and then saved into a spreadsheet program. With the rubric saved as a spreadsheet, the owner can make modifications to customize it by including headers, footers, or boxes for notations. He or she may also format the cells so that the text fits the space and is justified to his or her liking.

Another option is for teachers to use a word-processing program to generate a scale or rubric to match the teachers' expectations for the project. Such an example is displayed in Figure 8.2.

Figure 8.1 Example of an Evaluation Rubric Created Using Online Resources

Name: _____

	4. Distinguished	3. Proficient	2. Apprentice	1. Novice
Oral Presentation–Audience:				
Relates to topic, detailed, and accurate	All content directly related to the topic. Opinions were always supported by fact if possible.	Content directly related to the topic. Almost all opinions were supported by facts.	Demonstrated basic understanding of the topic. Many opinions were not supported by facts.	Few facts related to the topic. Most information was opinion.
Oral Presentation–Audience:				
Engage and interact with audience	Audience was engaged for entire presentation. Answered every question and comment.	Audience paid attention during most of presentation. Answered most audience questions.	Audience was interested for at least half of presentation. Tried to answer audience questions.	Audience lost interest at beginning of presentation. Could not answer audience questions.
Oral Presentation–Clarity:				
Clarity and volume	Spoke clearly so everyone could hear. Sounded interested in the topic. Changed voice to keep audience interested.	Spoke clearly so everyone could hear. Sounded interested in the topic.	Spoke quietly; increased volume after being asked. Sometimes did not sound interested in the topic.	Did not speak loud enough, even after being asked to speak up. Did not sound interested in the topic.
Oral Presentation–Props/Visual Aids:				
Relates to topic, high-quality, not distracting	Visual aids were high-quality and helped the audience understand the presentation.	Visual aids helped the audience understand the presentation.	Visual aids did not add to the presentation.	Visual aids missing or not complete.
Overall Score:				

Teacher Notes:

Figure 8.2 Example of an Evaluation Rubric Created Using a Word-Processing Program

---

A Light Story

Evaluation Form

Rating Scale:	Without a Doubt		Somewhat	Not at All	
	20	15	10	5	0

Student: _____   Date: _____

1. Story includes *reflection, refraction,* and *absorption.*	20	15	10	5	0
2. Story includes *transparent, translucent,* and *opaque.*	20	15	10	5	0
3. Story includes *color* and result of *change of lighting.*	20	15	10	5	0
4. Story has a *beginning, middle,* and *end.*	20	15	10	5	0
5. Story has correct *grammar, spelling,* and *punctuation.*	20	15	10	5	0

Teacher Notes: _____

_____

_____

Chapters 5 and 6 discussed the idea of using cloud storage systems, such as Schoology, to digitally house and maintain student work. This method of turning in, grading, and returning work puts a new spin on the idea of electronic portfolios. As mentioned, teachers who have students use cloud storage systems for their assignments can use electronic means to grade or evaluate student work. Each cloud storage learning management system (LMS) works a little differently. In general, students access and complete their assignments digitally, and upload them to an electronic folder. The teacher accesses the account to see who has completed the work and who has not. The teacher may also access student work to grade it, and then return it to students. This real-time evaluation method saves time; students do not have to wait one or two days or even a week to see how well they did on a particular assignment. (There is that highly effective instructional strategy of timely feedback coming into play again.) This information is quickly and easily typed into a conversation post and sent to students. Now, instead of using class time to explain what students can do to improve, discuss how to respond to particular answers, or clarify processes or ideas, the teacher can simply make adjustments to his or her lessons and move forward with instruction.

Using Technology to Create Rubrics for Evaluating Student Work: Benefits for Teachers and Students

- **Quick and easy to create.** Teachers can use ready-made rubrics, or quickly create their own using a database of criteria. Students can have access to the rubrics when assignments are presented, supporting their understanding of how their work will be evaluated.

- **Standardized criteria.** Teachers can select and use criteria statements from a database and repeat these same statements in subsequent rubrics. Students come to know the criteria and what they mean through repetition and standardization.

- **Easy revisions.** Teachers can quickly revise rubrics for future projects. Students can make suggestions for changes to criteria, which the teacher may incorporate immediately.

Conclusion

Teaching and learning are inextricably entwined in technology. Assessments and student evaluations of completed work provide balance to an effective educational experience grounded in technology. Formative and/or summative assessments may be online or digitally prepared. They may also include opportunities for students to use technology to demonstrate their understanding of concepts and skills by completing learning projects that require the use of computers or online resources. Whatever the assessment strategy or technique, technology brings a new dimension and ease to feedback for teachers. Teachers can know in real time how their students respond to content lessons. They can also use assessment software to analyze student outcomes. Online rubrics and scales provide teachers the support they need to design and implement meaningful, purposeful projects in which students will take pride.

Reflect and Respond

1. How do you see technology benefiting you and your students with regard to formative assessments?

2. How do you see technology benefiting you and your students with regard to summative assessments?

3. Set a goal for yourself. How do you intend to use technology or improve your use of technology for assessment purposes in the next two months?

4. When might you use a rubric to evaluate student learning? Create a rubric using a digital resource for a project you will assign to students in the near future.

Chapter 9

Classroom Management Tips and Strategies

If only teaching were as simple as developing a great lesson, teaching it, and watching all students master the content and leave that day smiling, happy, and satisfied. The real world of the classroom is not quite that simple. Day-to-day routines, processes, and procedures can sometimes interfere with instruction. There is also the matter of student behavior. Every class, it seems, has a student or a parent of a student who creates distractions that stifle learning opportunities for others in the class. Beginning teachers, in particular, struggle with classroom management, the foundational base of sound instruction. A teacher can have the best lesson, but without the ability to manage student behavior and classroom routines and processes, the lesson can fall flat and learning can be affected. Classroom management has long been correlated to student engagement, behavior, and instructional time, which directly affects student achievement (Wang, Haertel, and Walberg 1993). According to Linda Darling-Hammond in an interview with Marge Scherer (2012), the teaching profession needs teachers with "a combination of strong academic ability and the capacities to be very alert and attentive, to care about kids, to be able to understand what kids are doing and what they mean by it, and to manage classrooms and support children" (under "Do we really neeed the best and the brightest to enter the profession?"). This is no small feat for anyone, even the best and brightest teachers. Fortunately, with advances in communication and software, technology can lead teachers further into the 21st century feeling confident and capable as they continue to accomplish seventy-seven things at one time all day, every day.

Day-to-Day Processes

School is full of routines. Merriam-Webster Online Dictionary defines *routine* as "a regular way of doing things in a particular order." There are routines for morning drop-off, routines for the cafeteria, routines for students when they first enter the classroom, routines for turning in homework and class work—the list goes on and on. Our routines give order to what might otherwise be complete chaos. Routines are not bad, but they can become monotonous and boring. We can become so engrossed in our routines that we lose the excitement of learning, and one day at school becomes just like all the rest. The following sections highlight examples of how technology can ease the routines of day-to-day processes so that teachers may spend more time developing engaging, meaningful lessons for students.

> Teachers can download Common Core State Standards (CCSS) or state standards apps to their smartphones and tablets. These handy lesson-planning tools include quick references to the standards themselves as well as links to lesson plans, activities, and quizzes that teachers can use with students.

Lesson Plans

Technology can engage students by enlivening lessons and activities (Kuntz 2012). Howard Pitler et al. (2007) acknowledges that teachers who use technology can transform their classrooms into "dynamic learning environments" (2). This idea has been noted in the previous chapters. Technology can also streamline a teacher's routines, minimizing time spent on them while increasing time spent planning for and engaging students in learning activities. Utilizing technology for planning lessons enables teachers to take advantage of a host of features that make planning less burdensome and more creative. A familiar tool is to use word-processing or spreadsheet software to design lesson plan templates, which can be typed and saved in a documents folder. In either program, teachers can set the row and column heights and widths to suit their needs. By establishing a blank template, they can easily type and save plans from week to week, making only the modifications needed in the instructional boxes. Teachers can also link files, documents, and websites directly to their plans. This is especially helpful if teachers find the perfect website to share information or to play an online game related to the content that day. Then they need only open their lesson plans and click the link. It will take them (and their students) right to the site, making it both accessible and time-efficient.

Internet

Teachers can also use the Internet to search for and find online lesson plans related to a particular concept or topic. While some lessons are perfect just the way they are, others require simple adjustments to fit the needs of individual classrooms. By accessing lesson plans electronically, teachers can copy and paste them into a new word-processing document. Here the teacher may make the needed changes, and connect these revised plans to the "official" lesson planning document without having to reinvent the entire lesson from scratch. Web-based companies, such as netTrekker, The Teacher's Guide, and Teacher Tid Bytes, have assimilated the best educational resources specifically for teachers. By belonging to these systems, teachers, students, and parents can access instructional resources and learning tools that have been vetted by teachers. These types of sites rely on their reputation as sound, useful tools for day-to-day use, so teachers who become part of these systems know they have chosen reliable, worthy resources to support both teaching and learning.

Video Lessons

The idea of flipping classrooms and its benefits was discussed in Chapter 5 (Sams and Bergmann 2013). The Kentucky School Boards Association (2013) acknowledges the use of flipped classrooms as being beneficial not just to classroom teachers, but also to substitutes and absent students. An effective way to account for the clarity and effectiveness of instruction when teachers are away from their students is to provide saved video lessons that teach specific concepts. Teachers can feel confident about the content students receive in their absence where the same language and vocabulary from normal day-to-day routines is being used. Additionally, these same video lessons can aid students who were absent. Once provided access to the lesson, students can make up missed work with more confidence and understanding than when teachers may try to cram an entire day's content into a three-minute overview upon the student's return. Furthermore, students who need to revisit the lesson for a second or third time can easily do so.

Cloud Storage

Online storage plays an important role in a technology teacher's tool kit. Teachers who do not want to carry a computer back and forth from school can use a cloud storage system to save their plans. Then, by using any device with a hardwired or wireless Internet connection, they may access their plans anytime, anywhere. By accessing plans with embedded links to worksheets and websites, teachers have the whole package available, when they need it. This type of storage is not only beneficial to teachers; but students and their parents, and substitute teachers have quick access to reading assignments, spelling lists, morning work assignments, math problems, and graphic organizers. Also, teachers can easily assign remedial or enrichment work to students who need differentiation. Depending on the technology available, students can access their assignments from home or when they get to school, and complete them digitally or on paper, depending on their printing privileges or capabilities.

Assessments and Data Analysis

Another part of the planning process is the development, implementation, and follow-up of curriculum maps. Curriculum21 (2014) defines curriculum mapping as the process of organizing and maintaining a database of "operational curriculum." Curriculum includes instructional standards, such as those set forth by the Common Core State Standards. For example, a language arts teacher may focus on the development of informative/explanatory compositions for the first two months of school, then move on to narrative writing through December, and finally develop opinion/argument writing skills during the third semester. Embedded within these broader topics, there would be language skill lessons. This type of map provides long-range structure for instruction, and it allows teachers of the same content areas to check their progress not only in delivering the content, but also in the students' mastery of the learning objectives. The latter can be determined through the use of curriculum-based assessments developed specifically with the timeline in mind. Some teachers may refer to these as *common assessments*. Teachers within a grade-level team can use the same assessment tools throughout a course of study to determine where their own students are compared to the entire grade level. Teachers may use data charts or other analysis tools to help make meaning from countless test scores. This entire process amounts to a lot of organization of content, assessment, and student data.

Using Technology to Map Curriculum: Benefits for Teachers

- **Saves time in the long run.** Once curriculum maps are established, educators need only update them from year to year with current dates.

- **Builds collaboration among colleagues.** Ideally, teams of educators work together to construct curriculum maps. Technology can be used throughout the development of the maps as well as for distribution to all educators and to elicit feedback for improvements.

- **Links cross-curricular connections among content.** By using electronic databases, teachers can link instruction between and among content areas.

- **Links best-practices and effective instructional strategies.** Teachers can link valuable resources to support instruction to the mapped curriculum.

- **Links assessments.** Teachers can link common formative assessments to curriculum maps, ensuring that they stay on track with the instructional timeline as well as to check students' progress toward meeting the learning objectives.

It would be marvelous if one system or one program could masterfully maintain this information for us. The good news is, such programs exist. One is Super Duper Data Tracker by Super Duper Publications. Another is MasteryConnect, a full web-based program that will track both teacher and student progress through mapped standards, allow teachers to save and upload resources directly aligned to national standards, allow teachers to share common assessments for the standards, and scan and grade student responses to the common assessments. Schools or districts may have a similar web-based program of their own that enables teachers to use classroom assessment tools to understand what their students do and do not know. This allows teachers to make sound instructional decisions based on their students' needs. It also allows administrators to manage information for the benefit of making sound school- and district-based decisions by way of instructional resources and personnel.

Grading

Using Technology to Keep Track of Grades: Benefits for Teachers and Students

- **Monitor students' progress.** Teachers can customize grade books to visually display exemplary, satisfactory, and unsatisfactory grades. Teachers who use these systems can more quickly use students' grades to inform instruction, providing needed support and extensions for those who need them.

- **Set up standards-based grade books.** Teachers can customize their grade books to better reflect the instructional outcomes for each class or group(s) of students.

- **Custom weighting.** Teachers can use Excel formulas to "weight" grades.

- **Instant averages.** Teachers can set up Excel spreadsheets to average grades.

- **Email updates.** Teachers can email students or families grade updates by copying and pasting an entire row of grades into the body of an email.

- **Never lose a grade book.** By storing grades in a cloud-based system or on a school's secure server, teachers can be assured that their grade sheets will never "get lost."

Chapter 4 showed how students could learn to use spreadsheet software to make calculations and develop and analyze number patterns. This works for teachers, too. They can set up a spreadsheet program to calculate grade averages. Once grades are entered, the program runs the calculations and provides the class average automatically. Spreadsheet software is also helpful for managing student data, such as those already mentioned in the previous section. Teachers who administer school-level or district-level assessments can enter scores in a spreadsheet program that analyzes data for them. By assigning colors to cells based on the numbers entered, teachers can quickly scan the page to see which students grasp the concept thoroughly, which are struggling to understand it, and which are ready to move onto the next concept (see Figure 9.1).

Figure 9.1 Excel Spreadsheet with Color-Coded Cells Based on Students' Grades

Class Grades: Reading

TEACHER: Mrs. King

Student Name:	Classwork			Quizzes			Tests	
	12-Oct	23-Oct	30-Oct	13-Oct	24-Oct	31-Oct	20-Oct	3-Nov
Abby A.	95	92	100	88	95	90	83	92
Josh B.	94	85	80	70	75	85	85	85
Erin C.	72	70	75	75	88	80	76	80
Kelly D.	65	72	65	70	68	70	69	64
Geraldo H.	88	80	88	86	90	85	75	74
Class Average	83	80	82	78	83	82	78	79

Classroom management systems, grades, and data tracking can also be managed using software programs marketed specifically for these purposes, such as Easy Grade Pro and Gradekeeper. Some schools and districts now use secure online grading systems, which teachers can access using any computer or device that has Internet capabilities. Moreover, some programs provide passwords to parents and students so that they can access their classroom grades any time. This way, parents and students do not need to wait for formal interim or quarterly progress reports to see how they are doing.

Besides software programs, there are free online grading programs available to teachers. iGradePlus and MasteryConnect allow teachers to enter and maintain classroom data using secure online websites. Again, teachers do not need their school computers to access this information; they may do so from anywhere they have Internet access. The most challenging aspect of this entire online secure record keeping is that teachers may have multiple logins and passwords to remember. One solution is to keep an electronic document listing the sites or programs, and usernames and passwords for each. There is even an app for that, such as Password Gorilla, KeePass, and Passpack.

Teachers who are not quite ready to move to electronic grading systems can still use technology to facilitate grading. Groovy Grader, for instance, acts as an electronic version of the traditional cardboard grade calculator. Simply program the number of questions and click a few buttons to convert raw scores into grades.

Managing Classroom Behavior

Using Technology to Manage Student Behavior: Benefits for Teachers and Students

- **Keep track of positive and negative behaviors.** Teachers and students can set behavior goals and chart progress electronically. Periodic check-ins allow teachers to conference with students regarding their progress.

- **Graph academic achievement.** Teachers can make charts showing individual student and class progress over time. These visuals motivate students to out-perform their achievement on the next quiz or test.

- **Keep it fresh.** Teachers and students can use online programs to track student behavior, including the use of positive reinforcement for positive behavior.

- **Self-monitoring tools.** Teachers can use software apps, such as ClassDojo, to help students keep track of the classroom volume levels, and of their own actions in the classroom.

Teachers manage classroom behavior every moment that students are in their presence. Organizing the space, enforcing classroom expectations and consequences, following routines, and guiding students successfully through these takes a lot of effort throughout each day. It is not uncommon for a challenging student to try the patience of the most effective teachers. These students may have behavior modification plans, requiring teachers to collect and chart data based on the students' specific behavior goals. Spreadsheet software programs that graph data are instrumental for this purpose (Emmer et al. 2006). Teachers can use stem-and-leaf plots or multiple bar graphs to show when and how often a specific behavior occurs. Online programs can be helpful, such as PBIS World (Positive Behavioral Interventions and Supports) and School Wide Information System (SWIS). Additionally, teachers can use graphing software to motivate and encourage students to succeed in class (Grady 2011). A simple pie chart showing the breakdown of grades on a unit test may inspire students to perform better next time (see Figure 9.2). Teachers who have multiple classes of the same subject can drive a competition among classes to outperform one another. Students can maintain their own line graph showing the number of multiplication facts they can correctly answer or sight words they can correctly identify in one minute. The use of graphs for instructional purposes can increase intrinsic motivation in any classroom.

Figure 9.2 Pie Chart of Test Grades Earned by Class

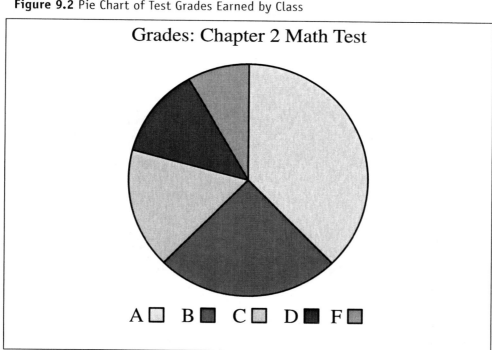

Using Technology Tools in Classroom Management

ClassDojo is a behavior management software program for the classroom. It is designed to help teachers maintain on-task student behavior. With it, teachers may reinforce positive class behavior and positive individual student behavior, and track (graph) behavior automatically (Scheie 2014). The best part is, any teacher can use it: classroom teachers, fine arts teachers, Exceptional Student Education (ESE) teachers, English language learner (ELL) teachers, elective teachers, and guidance counselors. The program comes ready to use with both positive and negative behaviors. Teachers need only add their students' names and additional behaviors, and then they are ready to Dojo. Teachers can select students and mark the preferred behavior. The program keeps track of everything and includes a home-school connection option where parents can log in and see how (and what) their child is (and is not) doing. This program works with computers and handheld devices. Teachers who maintain access to a smartphone throughout the day, no matter their location in the classroom, can monitor a whole class during independent work time or at a table for small-group instruction. The automated charts and graphs can be used for classroom review at the end of the day or week. Teachers may follow up with their usual rewards and consequences using the data safely stored in the system. They can also share reports with behavior intervention teams by simply pulling up a report.

ClassDojo keeps students engaged with regard to their behavior. Digital random selectors, digital timers, and volume control apps further help teachers and students be successful in the classroom. Digital random selectors can do the same with regard to students' classwork. Using apps that allow for random selection of students digitally replaces the old "popsicle-stick-in-a-can" routine. This simple classroom management strategy perks up students' interest and engagement. Likewise, teachers can use and display digital timers using their computer and projector to accurately and effectively implement the "classroom countdown." Students have a continuous visual to reference so that they may better manage their work time. There are modifications on this idea with various looks and displays for timers, including sand timers and traffic lights. Teachers can choose the app that works best for them, or they may download several to rotate through as the day or week progresses.

Busy classrooms tend to be noisy. Students talk, collaborate, share, and think out loud. Oftentimes, students exceed reasonable volume limits. It is easy for them to get caught up in what they are doing and for classroom protocols to go by the wayside. An app, such as Too Noisy Pro, can help teachers and students maintain an orderly classroom environment by sounding an alarm each time the noise level gets to be too much. These apps allow teachers to set the volume level within acceptable limits, and the program lets students know when the noise level exceeds those limits.

Video Recorded Lessons

As discussed previously, video recorded lessons have value for teachers, parents, students, substitutes, and administrators. They can also work to the teachers' (and students') advantage when used to monitor classroom behavior. Students tend to be their own best critics. Intervention Central, a website devoted to providing schools with the resources they need to help struggling learners and to effectively implement the Response to Intervention (RtI) model, offers this about teaching students self-monitoring techniques: "Self-monitoring takes advantage of a behavioral principle: the simple acts of measuring one's target behavior and comparing it to an external standard or goal can result in lasting improvement to that behavior" (under "Behavioral Interventions") Teachers who want to involve students in the problem-solving process by identifying a specific behavior to improve and then developing a plan for improvement may do so with the use of video recorded lessons. Pocket video cameras are inexpensive, small, and inconspicuous. Teachers can let their students know they are being recorded. Initially, behavior is likely to be exemplary; students do not want to be the first one who acts up on camera. Then, as the lesson progresses, routines set in and students forget about the camera. Students typically will act as they always do. When the class views the video, it is important that the teachers not allow anyone to "call out" another student—this exercise belongs to the whole class. If there were just one student with regular infractions, the teacher would handle it with just that one student. Students can independently note the behaviors that interfere with instruction. The class can come up with procedures, consequences, and rewards that will hopefully turn the behaviors into positive ones, improving the learning environment for everyone. This strategy also works well with individual students. Teachers can use video recording to target specific behaviors from specific students. This documentation may also help during parent conferences. A word of caution: Some schools or school districts may have policies regarding video recording students and the sharing of videos with parents. Teachers should check with an administrator before moving forward with this idea.

Digital Positive Motivators

To help motivate students to complete their homework (or classwork) and encourage better work habits, teachers can use digital positive motivators. Students love games, and they enjoy playing them at school. They also like to know that their efforts are noticed. Teachers can download formatted games, such as Monopoly, that work with interactive whiteboards, and use these as rewards for turning in completed homework (or any other behavior the teacher wants to target). As students enter the room, they see the teacher to turn in their work. Once their work is checked over, they may roll the digital die and move their game piece that many spaces. Instead of winning properties or railroads, the students are rewarded with more class-appropriate prizes, such as ten minutes of computer time, a pencil, or time to sit at the teacher's desk. In this instance, the board is an endless ring of positive reinforcement. The students can play all year long, as long as they do what is needed to earn the privilege of moving their game board piece.

Home-School Connection

Educators have known for many years that strengthening the home-school connection can benefit students academically, socially, and behaviorally. The research on this topic has been synthesized by Anne T. Henderson and Karen L. Mapp (2002) in "A New Wave of Evidence: The Impact of School, Family, and Community Connections on Student Achievement." In short, schools that welcome students' families, clarify misconceptions between teachers and parents, share resources, understand the home context, develop family involvement, and understand the role of the family can strengthen home-school relationships, recognition, and involvement. With so many people now having access to information through smart technologies, teachers are equipped to make pertinent classroom information available to families on school or class websites. With every home-school connection roadblock comes a new technology to overcome it. This section explores some options available to teachers to include and inform as many families as possible to maintain an open, friendly, caring climate of communication between school and home.

Classroom Websites

Classroom websites may take time initially to set up. However, once the sites are formatted, teachers may make simple adjustments from week to week. This provides students and their families with Internet access relevant classroom information, such as spelling and vocabulary lists, bulleted facts related to content topics, updates on field trips or other school events, homework assignments, and project deadlines. This type of communication system might take the place of a traditional weekly classroom newsletter. Alternatively, the weekly newsletter, also completed digitally using a template from a publishing program, can be embedded or linked to the classroom website. This communication tool is very helpful for families wanting to stay connected to their child's learning. When the website is updated and used consistently, students and their families know where to go for information and online resources to support instruction. Teachers can also add a link to their school email address so that families may email with quick questions or notes.

Wiki

A *wiki* is similar to a classroom website, except others may contribute to the information posted, and even edit or revise others' contributions. This type of site allows an entire classroom community of students, their families, and teachers to collaborate, share, and connect with others. Here, teachers (and students) can add information students need to know for tests or include practice problems that students can collaborate on to solve in preparation for the assessment. Postings may be added too, leading to a more complete and thoughtful information-gathering place. One advantage is that the teacher does not necessarily need to do all of the work. Students who thrive on challenges and cannot get enough of school will gladly add notes and information for others to use. This may be especially beneficial for developing vocabulary knowledge and usage. The teacher can post words and "official" definitions; students can add student-friendly definitions and sentences using words in context. Teachers interested in exploring the value of a classroom wiki can get started at Wikispaces, PBworks, or Zoho Wiki. Since this type of site is open to anyone who is included in the group, families can access information to help their children study and get a glimpse of what is happening in the classroom from the students' perspectives. This can work to strengthen communication between home and school, and help families feel that they are taking a more active role in their children's education.

Texting and Emailing

Using Technology to Communicate with Students and Families: Benefits for Teachers and Students

- **Instant messages.** Teachers can send instant messages about homework, projects, or field trip reminders to students and their families. This helps everyone stay up-to-date with daily/weekly/monthly events.

- **Important curriculum information.** Teachers can post assignments, links to tutorials, or even how-to videos, accessible to anyone with an Internet connection.

- **Anytime access to information.** Teachers can post information, such as newsletters, assignments, and a calendar of events, that is available 24-7. Students and families can ask relevant, time-sensitive questions and receive answers in record time.

The ease with which people communicate today is, at times, mind-boggling. Texting and emailing seem to be more normal than calling or talking in person. It should seem natural, then, that teachers prefer to use text and email to communicate with families. With all of the features of both types of media, teachers have many options from which to choose to find just the right fit for them so home-school communication remains open. Some teachers are perfectly comfortable providing their personal cell phone numbers to student families so that they may call with questions, comments, or concerns at any time. Other teachers may not be so forthcoming with this information. Schools or districts may have policies regarding the use of personal cell phones during student contact hours, which is equally as problematic if this is the most effective means of communicating with student families. Some teachers communicate best individually with student families through school email. By setting up a student family group at the start of the school year, teachers can send reminders or notices to all student families at one time, rather than individually. Another option is to use an online texting service, such as

Remind 101. This program works like any text messaging service. Messages can be sent to cell phones or email addresses. The advantage is that teachers can text information quickly to a large group of people at one time. Also, teachers do so through a third party, so their personal cell information is kept personal.

Online Gradebook Programs

With online security improving, student families now have the option of logging in to see their child's progress in their academic courses. Professional online gradebook programs offer login accounts for teachers, students, and their families. These systems are typically purchased and directed through the school district. They provide student families with constant access to their children's graded tests, quizzes, and classwork. As a teacher enters grades, this information becomes immediately available for students (if they, too, have a login account) and their families. With this type of system, student families no longer need to wait for paper interim or end-of-grading-period report cards. They may log on to see their child's grades at any time throughout the grading period and throughout the school year.

Conclusion

Technology can make teachers' lives easier, not only by way of curriculum and instruction, but also through planning and management of resources, assessments, classroom routines, and student behavior. Using technology, teachers can administer assessments, record the results, and access and analyze the data with ease on their own time. This is most useful for teachers who use assessment results to drive instructional decisions and modify lesson plans to meet students' needs.

Reflect and Respond

1. What day-to-day processes and procedures has technology made easier for you? What else might you use to help make routine tasks even easier?

2. How do you see technology supporting your efforts to maintain an orderly classroom environment? How might this translate into improved student behavior?

3. Explain how technology can help strengthen and support the home-school connection.

4. What do you see as the greatest value technology has to offer with regard to managing time, space, and people?

Chapter 10

Professional Development to Strengthen Technology Integration

Some teachers are self-directed. They have a natural talent for seeking out, finding, and using the most current instructional strategies, materials, and techniques with their students, and they do so with enthusiasm and confidence. They know instinctively what engages learners, and they meet new challenges head on with robust vigor. Some teachers rely on others (e.g., leaders, coaches, colleagues, and specialists) to point them in the right direction and provide models and examples of the strategies, techniques, and materials that make good teachers great. Some teachers lack confidence with and/or acceptance of techniques and strategies that would maximize student learning. Regardless of where they are, all teachers can benefit from meaningful, relevant, and purposeful professional development. In fact, the highest-achieving nations on international measures, such as the PISA (Programme for International Student Assessment) and TIMSS (Trends in International Math and Science Study), are intent on developing teachers' expertise throughout their careers (Wei, Andree, and Darling-Hammond 2009).

Most teachers respond favorably to new and better ways of doing things with the support of their colleagues and administrations. Teaching is not an independent activity. It takes collaboration, community, and encouragement from all stakeholders. Linda Darling-Hammond's research (2010) on effective schools found that among the five practices employed by highly effective schools, highly competent teachers who collaborate in planning and problem solving ranked among them. Interestingly, the International Society for Technology in Education (ISTE) has identified fourteen essential conditions necessary to effectively leverage technology for learning. Among them is ongoing professional learning. This chapter explores options for schools that are looking for ways to provide sustained, relevant professional development in the area of technology to keep teacher learning moving forward in a positive direction, evidenced by increased student engagement and mastery of content.

Getting the Most from Professional Development

Just as teachers develop lesson plans to maximize student learning, leaders in charge of professional development should have a clear road map of what they want their teachers to learn, including objectives, outcomes, activities, and evaluation tools. Any professional development endeavor is only as effective as its plan. Simply putting ideas on paper and going through the motions without follow-up will lead to confusion and frustration, and ultimately, nothing will change. Teachers use formative and summative assessments to determine the extent to which their students learn the content presented, and professional development leaders should do the same. However, their assessment will likely be in the form of observation and follow-up discussion rather than an actual assessment.

A professional development plan may entail long-range goals and objectives, or it may be more time sensitive. Figure 10.1 shows an example of a long-range technology plan for a small school (about 500 students) just beginning to build its technology base. This type of plan will lay the foundation for individual professional development sessions where teachers learn to effectively incorporate the technology provided. For example, once the school purchases interactive whiteboards (IWBs), school leaders will want to plan professional development sessions related to both basic and advanced uses of this powerful learning tool. Figure 10.2 illustrates how a plan may look for the IWB sessions related to the long-range plan in year two.

Figure 10.1 Example of a Long-Range Technology Plan

Technology	End of Year 1	End of Year 2	End of Year 3	End of Year 4
Hardware	One 25-station computer lab; 3 eReaders per grade level; 3 wireless printers	12 eReaders per grade level; 8 wireless printers; 5 IWBs	Two 25-station computer labs; 15 eReaders per grade level; 12 wireless printers; 3 sets of student response systems	3 eReaders per classroom; 10 IWBs; 6 sets of student response systems
Software	adequate licenses for instructional support programs	individualized programs; typing program	individualized programs	teacher accounts for online instructional support
Infrastructure	adequate server space and bandwidth	schoolwide wireless network		
Other	technology fair*; before- and after-school lab sessions; online grade program	Family Technology Night	technology-related competitions	technology summer camp

*For ideas to present at a technology fair visit http://www.sciencekids.co.nz/projects/technology.html, http://www.education.com/science-fair/computers/, and http://cawthronsciencefair.org.nz/Ideas+and+Help.

Figure 10.2 Example of an Outline for a Single- or Multiple-Session In-Service

Topic: Interactive Whiteboards
Content Map

Stage 1 – Desired Results

Goal:
Teachers will have a working knowledge of how to use an interactive whiteboard (IWB) for instructional and assessment purposes.

Understandings: Teachers will understand that IWBs are a worthwhile investment; IWBs can increase student engagement; and there are plenty of ready-made resources available for them to use with their IWBs.	**Essential Question:** How can teachers best use the basic and advanced features of an IWB to increase student achievement in all subject areas?
Teachers will know how to organize their classroom to maximize the IWB's potential and to whom they may turn when simple problems become more complex.	**Teachers will be able to** hook up and start their IWB, troubleshoot simple problems, create and find meaningful activities to support instruction, and use basic and advanced features for both instruction and assessment.

Stage 2 – Assessment Evidence

Performance Tasks:	**Other Evidence:**
• Teacher-made IWB activities • Lesson plans	• Participation • Discussion • Observation • Student achievement

Stage 3 – Learning Plan

Learning Activities:

- Interactive whiteboard basics: tools and features

- Create and use interactive activities with whiteboard templates

- Find and use interactive activities posted by other teachers

- Use the adopted programs' interactive activities

- Use advanced IWB features

- Use connected student response systems for formative and summative assessments

- Determine next steps (future purchases, future workshop sessions, follow-up)

Barbara B. Levin and Lynne Schrum (2013) identified eight key characteristics of schools that successfully use technology. One of these is strong and distributed school leadership. Teachers need to know, feel, and see what their administrations expect, and know that they will be following up to ensure teachers are meeting these expectations. Thoughtful encouragement, support, and recognition can motivate teachers to continue moving forward, in spite of the challenges they may face, especially when using technology. For example, a school or district that expects teachers to use a particular online or student response system must put the structures in place to:

- ensure that the assessments are administered;

- provide technology support if needed to administer the assessments;

- make the meaning and usefulness of the results transparent; and

- devise strategies that use the results to lead to improved student achievement.

Omission of any one of these must-dos may lead teachers to believe that their time is not valued and that using the technology has no merit. A lack of commitment on the part of a school or district's leadership will ultimately lead to a lack of commitment on the part of the teachers. Levin and Schrum (2013) describe several examples to demonstrate how school and district leaders support technology integration in schools. In one example, the district "provided a technology facilitator and a help desk at every school, often staffed by students. Tech facilitators suggested and modeled new tools" (53). This support allowed teachers to try new things without the fear of failure. They go on to say that teachers felt supported by their administrators, who were enthused and encouraged their teachers to explore and take risks.

Teachers who feel a sense of ownership in their own professional development will likely yield greater learning and application of new and different skills, techniques, models, and resources than teachers who are told what to do regardless of their interests or personal needs for development (Witherspoon 1989; Education World 2014). Not all teachers need training related to technology integration; some naturally seek, find, and use the tools available to them with students, and they do so expertly, always remembering that the goal of any instructional idea is to improve literacy or math skills, or to understand complex content-area topics and related information. These teachers are leaders in their own right. Their resourcefulness and enthusiasm can be used to encourage others to follow suit. Needs assessments allow teachers to feel as if their interests matter, especially when they see evidence of school and district leaders providing support for the topics requested. An example of a technology-based professional development needs assessment is shown in Figure 10.3. A school can demonstrate the usefulness of online surveys by creating one with these questions and providing the link to teachers instead of printing hard copies (and having to manually evaluate them).

Figure 10.3 Sample Technology-Based Professional Development Needs Assessment

Please help us determine our professional development needs related to technology integration. Your thoughtful, honest feedback will help us plan professional development sessions to support and extend our school's needs. Thank you!

1. How often do you use technology for professional purposes, such as writing lesson plans, collaborating with other teachers, or finding information to extend your own learning?

   ( ) every day   ( ) weekly   ( ) monthly   ( ) hardly ever

2. How often do you use technology for instructional purposes, such as teaching content, assessing students, or engaging students in independent/paired/small-group technology tasks?

   ( ) every day   ( ) weekly   ( ) monthly   ( ) hardly ever

3. Which technology do you see **best** benefiting you with regard to the content you teach?

   ( ) Internet or other online content resources

   ( ) Internet or other online professional development videos, blogs, or chat rooms

   ( ) Common and shared lesson plans within our school

   ( ) Common and shared content resources

   ( ) Word-processing, spreadsheet, and desktop-publishing software

   ( ) Other _____

4. Which technology do you see **best** benefiting your students with regard to the content you teach?

   ( ) Internet or other online content resources

   ( ) Interactive whiteboard or similar device

   ( ) Individual handheld devices with wireless Internet support

   ( ) Content-related software programs

   ( ) Other _____

5. Which of the following technology-related options **best** defines the professional development sessions you would like to see more?

- ⬭ Learning about curriculum and instructional resources
- ⬭ Using interactive games and activities to support content
- ⬭ Using online assessments
- ⬭ Managing student data, files, and resources
- ⬭ Using student response systems (premade and teacher-made tests)
- ⬭ Using interactive whiteboards
- ⬭ Using handheld devices
- ⬭ Using online research tools with students
- ⬭ Other _____

6. What do you find to be the greatest challenge with regard to integrating technology into the curriculum?

Utilization of Resources: Time, People, and Things

Time is a precious commodity. This is especially true in the classroom, and no one knows this better than teachers. Finding time for professional development can be challenging. However, if the professional development plan has a clear focus, a clear long-range vision, and clear and expected outcomes, teachers will see the value in it and devote the time they need to master these new skills, strategies, and techniques. Teachers want to know that their time is valued and that their professional development will lead to increased learning in the classroom. The professional development models and methods in the next sections are aimed at maximizing teacher learning while respecting the time they will need to invest in it for the benefit of their students. As a professional development plan develops, leaders should consider the time teachers will need to invest and demonstrate the costs and benefits of this investment. Meaning, teachers will want to know that the four hours they spend engaged in a particular professional development session or series of sessions will yield equitable results by saving them time in the long run and/or by advancing their students' learning by X amount.

People are another precious commodity in the world of education. As budgets get cut, so do positions. However, the workload never diminishes despite the reduced personnel. It is prudent for schools and school districts to mindfully spend their dollars. Given the numerous benefits to using technology in instruction (Cheung and Slavin 2012; Tamim et al. 2011; Means et al. 2009), someone needs to be available with technical support when glitches and breakdowns occur. This could be a school- or district-based liaison, online or telephone technology support or help desk, on-staff technology coaches, or other professionals who may assist as needed throughout the day and around the building. Equally important is the availability of designated technology staff to ensure ample instructional support as well as the visibility and encouragement of administrators and other school leaders of teachers who frequently incorporate technology into their instruction. Small notes, brief comments, or accolades in a weekly or monthly school newsletter offer kind words of encouragement and help teachers feel that their bosses recognize and value the efforts they make to use technology with their students.

Can a school have too much technology? Maybe. It can certainly have too much underutilized technology. More likely, teachers may feel their school lacks adequate hardware, software, and/or infrastructure (wireless networking, data storage, and personnel) for them to effectively integrate technology into the school day. The school's technology integration plan will help maintain a guided focus on the devices and programs necessary for full and effective implementation. (Suggestions for acquiring adequate resources are offered in Chapter 1.) Regardless of the quantity of available resources, school leaders should realize that without an investment in time and people, even the most state-of-the-art technology might sit idle. The best means of encouraging the use of available technology is for workshop providers to use the technology and have teachers use the technology they expect to see students using in the classroom. Teachers who bring portable devices or laptops to trainings can take notes, make instant posts to school wikis or blogs, and immediately use the instructional resources that they are being shown. The more engaged teachers are with the technology provided, the more capable they will become with it, and the more likely they will be to use it and use it well while teaching.

Logistics

Oftentimes, schools need to share technology, such as portable labs, handheld devices, computer lab time, and limited licenses of purchased programs. A designated technology teacher, coach, or paraprofessional can work along with administration to develop an equitable plan for all teachers. For example, an elementary school with two portable netbook labs will have to use creative scheduling to accommodate fifty classroom teachers. Again, the school's instructional and/or technology plan should provide direction. If students consistently score poorly in mathematics but adequately in language arts, these devices may only be shared among math teachers at certain grade levels, or they may rotate through grade levels during math blocks throughout the day. In this case, teachers would need training in how to maximize the time their students have to interact with the tablets to hone math skills and solve math problems relevant to their current focus of study. Simply using these devices for students to practice basic computation facts may boost students in this one skill area, but it will not maximize the usefulness that these devices can offer students in the long run.

The balance of time, people, and resources is delicate. School leaders should remember throughout any technology-related professional development that the technology is a means to an end. Having a clear purpose for professional development that teachers are a part of creating will help them see the value in it. As a result, they will be eager to invest in learning about the most current strategies, methods, and techniques as related to their situations. Supporting teachers with people who can help keep things moving is also essential. Knowing what is available, what is hot, and what is pertinent to the school's overall objectives will help keep a steady pace for acquiring needed technology and using it equitably and meaningfully through the school year.

Professional Development Models

Professional development takes time. A variety of options exist to attend sessions, such as off-hours, before or after the school, on Saturdays, over the summer months, or during on-contract time, which may require a substitute in the classroom. Any of these options may also require travel, an expense many schools may be restricting or omitting. The most cost-effective means of providing professional development is when teachers volunteer their time to participate in off–hour sessions. However, depending on the topic, these types of sessions may impose time limitations that do not make them feasible. Also, depending on contract negotiations, teachers may not be compelled to attend. There is no single time–management method that is best for any one school or district. Any single planned training event will not meet everyone's needs. However, with a model for sustained professional development over an extended period of time, schools can schedule professional development events that hopefully reach a wide range of teachers' needs. Professional development sessions should also maximize the time that teachers are engaged with a particular topic. Some topics may take just a few minutes, whereas others might take several hours to master. Figure 10.4 shows how one school's long–range professional development plan might look based on the infrastructure of the school and training needs of the staff.

Figure 10.4 Sample Long-Range Professional Development Plan

Year	Timeline	Topics	Models and Methods
1	Monthly for initial trainings; as needed for follow-up, extension, and review sessions	Schoolwide instructional programs	30- to 45-minute small-group sessions during early release days and as needed during planning periods and/or before and after school; online tutorials
	Before start of school year	Online grading program	45-minute pre-service whole-school workshop; follow-up with 2x quarterly during grade-level meetings
2	4x annually	eReader share-out of successes and challenges	Peer-led discussions during monthly staff meetings
	Monthly for initial trainings; as needed for follow-up, extension, and review sessions	Interactive whiteboards; interactive instructional technology	30- to 45-minute small-group sessions during early release days and as needed during planning periods and/or before and after school; online tutorials
3	Monthly	eReaders	Professional learning community

On-Contract Professional Development

One common practice among school districts is to allow early-release days designated for professional development. Once each week, month, or quarter, students are dismissed early, and teachers remain on campus (or go off campus) to attend a professional development session. Neighboring schools may collaborate to offer varied in-services, and teachers may choose to attend the session that applies to them. Alternatively, schools may participate in professional learning communities, where teachers collaborate with others to decide on a topic to discuss, plan for, and follow through with as the school year progresses. For example, middle school science teachers might work on using their limited in-class computers and/or lab time to enroll students in their textbook company's online testing program and try this option as a means of summative assessment. Another example is third grade reading teachers who collaborate to write common comprehension test questions in their school's student response system program, eliminating the need for paper-and-pencil tests. In both examples, the team of teachers collaborates with an end product in mind, a focus for the group, and a means of ensuring that everyone on the team follows through with his or her responsibilities to the team effort.

Other on-contract professional development models include using whatever time is available before or after school. These workshop sessions can be organized to target small groups of teachers or an entire staff. Professional development during planning periods allows technology leaders to check in with teachers regarding specific technology or provide mini-lessons on programs, strategies, and processes that affect student outcomes and help teachers manage their own time and resources. Finally, schools may pull teachers together for longer periods of time during the school day by offering class coverage either through school-based personnel (paraprofessionals, resource teachers, or administrators) or substitute teachers. This latter option bears extra cost, but for topics that require extended time frames, presenters can deliver the necessary information in one setting. One idea to maximize in-school time is to have roving substitutes. For example, a workshop may be anticipated to take about two hours. This amounts to about three sessions during the entire eight-hour school day, including breaks, transition time, and lunch. Six subs would release six teachers first thing in the morning, and then rotate to the next six teachers, making the last transition. In this one day and for the cost of six substitutes, eighteen teachers would be able to receive a complete workshop related to an essential piece of technology.

Off-Contract Professional Development

Sometimes, schools just cannot squeeze in all of the professional development teachers need during the school year or during the school day. In these cases, schools may have no choice but to move professional development workshops into off-contract time, when teachers are not required to be in attendance. This presents challenges related to getting information out to all teachers since they are not contractually obligated to attend and cannot be compelled to do so. Incentives, such as stipends, raffles or drawings for big-ticket items, or the promise of extra classroom money, materials, or equipment, can coax some teachers into attending workshops that do not take place during the school day or school year. Representatives from larger companies who present workshops can usually provide prizes or giveaways at no cost to schools. Then again, some teachers do not need any incentive at all. Provide the training, and they will come. Administrators and professional development coordinators should act to make the best decisions for their districts and schools to reach the most teachers in the time allocated when needing to extend professional development opportunities beyond contract time.

Summertime professional development opportunities, such as workshops, institutes, and conferences, allow teachers to stay current on their own time, during a time when they have many fewer responsibilities toward students, parents, and administrators. Sessions that take place earlier in the summer allow teachers to assimilate information more carefully and completely, giving them time to try out different facets of the trainings without feeling rushed or pushed. Sessions that take place later in the summer, closer to the beginning of the school year, limit the time teachers have to process, practice, and assimilate the information. Conversely, teachers have less time to forget or lose the information during the hustle and bustle of the start of the school year.

Saturday workshops are another viable option for schools to provide extended learning opportunities for teachers. However, these are usually less desirable due to personal commitments and responsibilities. However, when available, teachers might be willing to invest one or two hours on a Saturday to extend their own professional learning. As with any option, incorporating teacher preference into the time it is offered will go a long way in making it well attended.

Professional Development Methods

Models of professional development in technology are important. They define the time limitations and overall scope of training based on a school's technology integration plan. Once the model is decided upon, workshop facilitators may begin outlining the style of delivery that will best reach their target audience. Whichever methods they choose, the facilitators should provide thorough explanations, engaging activities, and essential follow-up to maximize the impact of the professional development sessions.

Digital Professional Development Options

Online professional development is bountiful, and most of what is posted is quite helpful. Teachers can find all kinds of relevant, meaningful, and short video clips online where real classroom teachers in real classroom situations demonstrate. Teachers might find clips on ways to use an interactive whiteboard more creatively or to provide adequate time for students to type stories and essays in class using limited classroom computers and lab time. These videos are available on YouTube and TeacherTube, and through other online professional resources. For example, PBS LearningMedia has a video related to flipped classrooms, among other topics. THE Journal has interactive information, including videos related to the preparation of online testing. Individual teachers might also have posted or linked clips to a personal or professional website, or clips might be mentioned in a technology blog that a teacher is following. An example of this is Web 2.0 Guru. This site has all kinds of tips, tricks, and information for teachers wanting to use the tools of the 21st century. Videos are also available through textbook publishers and other online organizations. The textbook a teacher has and uses now may provide essential professional development videos showing strategies and techniques in the classroom.

Webinars

Aside from teacher demonstration videos, publishers also offer *webinars*, or live educational presentations. Typically, while the presentation runs on a participant's computer, he or she may speak into the computer's microphone or type into a chat field to interact immediately with the presenter to ask questions, make comments, or clarify information. The webinar may have a call-in feature, so the presenter's voice comes over the intercom system of a telephone. In this case, the webinar is presented through the computer, but the audio comes through a phone line, where participants can participate. Some webinars are recorded, and teachers can access them at a later time to get or review the information. The downside to these is that they are no longer interactive between presenter and participants. Webinars are usually professionally done, presented by leaders in the field, and come to schools through respected organizations, such as the International Reading Association (IRA) and the International Society for Technology in Education (ISTE). Companies, such as Discovery Education and TIME for Kids, also provide thoughtful, relevant, and meaningful webinars on a variety of technology-related topics.

The best part about online video teacher training is that it usually can be delivered in a short time frame, and teachers can huddle in a team leader's classroom or other area with their peers as long as they have the necessary equipment: computer, projector, sound system, and (possibly) phone with intercom. When provided with focus questions and allowed to debrief and discuss the information, teachers can get a lot of information in a short period of time and have time to collaborate and assimilate the information to impact their students' learning.

Full Courses

Teachers wanting more in-depth training on a particular topic can take to the web for full courses related to a topic of particular interest. Seeing Math has integrated face-to-face and online interaction with web-based learning, video case studies, and interactive software to develop courses by teams of experts in math education and educational technology. PBS TeacherLine has a wide offering of online professional development courses for teachers. Drexel University has a math forum where teachers collaborate in a relaxed environment with researchers, students, parents, and other teachers to learn math and improve math education. Also, organizations, such as the National Council for Teachers of Mathematics (NCTM), the National Education Association (NEA), and the Association for Supervision and Curriculum Development (ASCD), provide online workshops and courses related to any number of technology topics. Some come with a cost, but members of these organizations can usually access courses for free or at a reduced fee.

Personal Professional Development Options

Of course, online professional development is not for everyone. Some teachers still learn best with and prefer face-to-face contact. The good news is, any of the models previously described will offer teachers this option. Teacher leaders, technology teachers, community members, and software and hardware representatives can all provide engaging workshops while offering the personal touch many teachers crave.

Professional Learning Communities

Another option for face-to-face professional development is the implementation of *professional learning communities* (PLCs). Richard DuFour (2004) states that PLCs maintain the assumption that students come to school to learn (versus coming to school to be taught). In order to achieve this, teachers understand that they must collaborate to ensure optimal learning for all students. Finally, discussions and regular team meetings are focused on and increased student outcomes. Once all three of these big ideas are in place, schools are engaged in true professional learning communities. Related to integrating technology, a PLC would still maintain these big ideas. Whatever technology a group of teachers is learning, they continuously return to the questions, "How is it impacting student learning?" and "How do we know?" A teacher leader, a curriculum leader, an administrator, or anyone who can guide the group to stay focused on student outcomes may lead a PLC. With the advent of cloud storage, PLCs can practice what they preach by going digital with meeting agendas, data analysis, instructional resources, and follow-up activities.

Learning communities may take place digitally, too. Here, teachers continue their collaboration but on their own time and at their own pace. Digital learning communities offer the PLC meeting without the actual meeting. Teachscape, based in San Francisco, offers support for school-based learning communities with online components. These include student work samples, assessment data, professional articles, and teacher videos. Stephen Sawchuk (2009) interviewed Maryann R. Marrapodi, Teachscape's chief learning officer who said, " 'When a professional learning community is set up within a school, there is often a limited amount of time. Through the online platform, they can continue their discussions anytime they want. It is an enhancement and extension, rather than an obstacle' " (under "Teacher").

Book Studies

Closely related to PLCs are book studies. Perhaps you are bringing one to a close right now, and this chapter is the final phase in the process of learning about instructional technology skills, strategies, programs, and techniques. Book studies have flexible schedules since the participants set their own timeline and determine when and where to meet. Ideally, book studies would involve all of the participants, requiring some task, such as trying out one idea and bringing feedback or evidence of student learning back to the group at the next meeting. Participants usually read a chapter or section of a book ahead of meeting so that they can have conversations about the information, problem solve, and clarify what is written, what is meant by what is written, and how it applies to the classroom setting. Given the usefulness of technology itself, perhaps a book study group has gone digital, and teachers who participate find resources centered on a particular topic, such as differentiated math. Then, when the book study group meets, teachers spend time sharing what they have discovered online, explaining how they were able to use the information in their classrooms. By using cloud storage or a wiki, teachers can post only the best of integrated instructional technology resources and tools in one place for others to locate and access quickly and easily when they need them.

Workshops and Conferences

Companies that manufacture and provide instructional materials specifically for schools may also include face-to-face workshops or training sessions with purchases of equipment or software. Some training may be provided with the school or district purchase; other training may require a fee. Consultants for technology companies operate similarly to consultants for textbook companies. They will come to schools for a day or two at a time to introduce, model, and teach teachers about their system and how it works in the classrooms. Generally, these sessions are a half or full day of training.

Conferences and institutes are large-scale events that can last several days. Concurrent breakout sessions may range between forty-five minutes to an hour each, or they may be scheduled for longer periods of time. On the vendor floor, companies demonstrate and sell their products to interested consumers. Teachers who attend in groups have a chance to learn professionally off campus, giving them the opportunity to collaborate. As grand as these events are, they come with a cost. Registration fees can run upward of hundreds of dollars, and there may be travel costs involved if the conference is not close by or teachers live and work in a more rural setting. The benefit is that teachers can attend sessions and hear presentations from keynote speakers who are experts in their fields. These small opportunities can have long-lasting impacts.

Something fairly new on the scene is the *unconference*. These smaller-scale conferences are participant driven. They involve little to no cost and have no registration process. They are organized, facilitated, and run exclusively by members of a school district, school site, or other educational organization. The idea is that teacher leaders completely control and run their own sessions on their own time, allowing for collaboration among colleagues and total participation from those who attend.

Teachers might also be familiar with *job-alike sessions*, where the room is organized with a large circle of chairs and the facilitator poses one question to the group. Every teacher has the opportunity to respond to the question, giving everyone the chance to learn from each other in a collaborative, supportive environment filled with teachers interested in hearing what their colleagues have to say. Both of these ideas have great potential in the area of instructional technology integration. Since technology moves so quickly and may seem nearly impossible to keep up with, teachers who attend a technology unconference can learn what works and what does not work, and hear stories and ask questions from those they admire most, their peers.

Conclusion

As illustrated in this chapter, simply having the most current technology available does not guarantee its effective use in classrooms. School leaders must ensure that teachers are equipped with the skills they need to integrate digital technologies and new approaches successfully into their teaching. They must also set a clear expectation that no teacher should ignore the importance of technology in learning. Schools with a strong supportive administration, those with an able-bodied technology support base, and those that ensure adequate time for targeted professional development based on short- and long-range technology implementation plans will reap the rewards that technology can bring over the long run. Schools should provide ongoing, meaningful, relevant, timely, and time-sensitive professional development to teachers based on the school's instructional needs and by having clear goals related to how technology can help the school accomplish its objectives.

"Professional Development to Stregthen Technology Integration" can be quickly summed up using the five *W*s and one *H*.

- **Who?** Who will benefit from technology-related professional development? Who will provide this professional development to teachers and staff?

- **What?** What topics will the professional development cover? What technology will teachers use as they learn a new skill, process, or program? What will the professional development look like?

- **Where?** Where will the professional development sessions take place?

- **When?** When will professional development sessions take place? What time of year and time during the day are best?

- **Why?** Why is this training needed for teachers to be able to advance students' academic achievement?

- **How?** How will the sessions be organized: whole staff, small group, or individual? How many sessions are needed, and how long will each session take? How will teachers benefit from these sessions? How will workshop presenters and/or school leaders follow up to ensure effective implementation of the information? How will teachers request and receive additional support or follow-up on an individual basis?

Reflect and Respond

1. What are your greatest technology-related professional development needs right now?

2. Go online and find a course, video, webinar, blog, or other professional development opportunity related to your specific needs.

3. Participate in the online training you discovered. Invite another teacher to join you. Reflect on the information. How will it impact your classroom?

4. Use a technology format (blog, website, post, or email) to share what you learned with another colleague. Explain how your investment in your own professional development related to technology has or will positively impact the academic achievement of your students.

Teacher Resources

Online Resources

Almost a Third Grader
http://www.almostathirdgrader.com

Amazing Alex
https://itunes.apple.com/us/app/amazing-alex-hd/id524334658 (Apple)
or https://play.google.com/store/apps/details?id=com.rovio.amazingalex.trial&hl=en (Android)

Animoto
http://animoto.com

ArtBabble
http://www.artbabble.org

Artifact
https://artifact.unboundconcepts.com

ArtsEdge
http://artsedge.kennedy-center.org/educators.aspx

Association for Library Service to Children (ALSC)
http://www.ala.org/alsc/

BBC Schools
http://www.bbc.co.uk/schools/scienceclips/

Blabberize
http://blabberize.com

Blogger
http://www.blogger.com

Box
https://app.box.com

BrainPOP and BrainPOP Jr.
http://www.brainpop.com and http://www.brainpopjr.com

BubbleSheet app
https://itunes.apple.com/us/app/bubblesheet/id413937393?mt=8

Center for Innovation in Engineering and Science Education (CIESE)
http://www.ciese.org/collabprojs.html

CK-12 Foundation
http://www.ck12.org/student

ClassDojo
http://www.classdojo.com

Classics for Kids
http://www.classicsforkids.com

Classtools.net
http://www.classtools.net

Coach's Eye
http://www.coachseye.com

Colonial Williamsburg
http://www.history.org

Criterion Online Writing Evaluation System
http://www.ets.org/criterion

Cyberbee
http://www.cyberbee.com/projects.html

Diigo
https://www.diigo.com

Discovery Education
http://www.discoveryeducation.com

DK Publishing
http://us.dk.com

easel.ly
http://www.easel.ly

EasyGradePro
http://www.easygradepro.com

eBackpack
https://www.ebackpack.com

EBSCO
http://search.ebscohost.com

Edmodo
https://www.edmodo.com

Edublogs
http://edublogs.org

Emily Dickinson Museum
http://www.emilydickinsonmuseum.org

Energyville
http://www.energyville.com

ePals
http://www.epals.com

ePub Bud
http://www.epubbud.com

e-rater
http://www.ets.org/erater/about

Exploratorium
http://www.exploratorium.edu

Flash card apps
https://itunes.apple.com/us/app/flashcards*/id403199818?mt=8 (Apple)
or https://play.google.com/store/apps/details?id=com.ichi2.anki&hl=en
(Android)

Funbrain
http://www.funbrain.com

Gaggle
https://www.gaggle.net

GeoGebra
http://www.geogebra.org/cms/en/

Gizmos
http://www.explorelearning.com

Global SchoolNet
http://www.globalschoolnet.org

Glogster EDU
http://www.glogster.com

Google Story Builder
http://docsstorybuilder.appspot.com

Google Translate
http://translate.google.com

Gradekeeper
http://www.gradekeeper.com

Grant Wrangler
http://www.grantwrangler.com

Highlights
https://www.highlights.com

HowStuffWorks
http://www.howstuffworks.com

iBooks app
http://www.apple.com/ibooks

Iditarod
http://iditarod.com

iGradePlus
https://www.igradeplus.com

Incredibox
http://www.incredibox.com

Infogr.am
http://infogr.am

IXL
http://www.ixl.com

JASON Learning
http://www.jason.org

Kenn Nesbitt's Poetry for Kids
http://www.poetry4kids.com

Kentucky Virtual Library for Kids Research Portal
http://www.kyvl.org/kids/homebase.html

Khan Academy
http://www.khanacademy.org

KidsClick!
http://www.kidsclick.org

Kidzworld
http://www.kidzworld.com

Kindle app
http://www.amazon.com

LaunchPad
http://www.classlink.com/launchpad/

LEGO
http://education.lego.com/

Library of Congress
http://www.loc.gov/index.html

Little Golden Books by Random House
http://www.randomhousekids.com/brand/little-golden-books/

MasteryConnect
http://www.masteryconnect.com

Math Forum
http://mathforum.org

Math Play
http://www.math-play.com

Math Playground
http://www.mathplayground.com

Mimio
http://www.mimio.com

Molecular Workbench
http://mw.concord.org/modeler/

Monkey Machine
http://www.rinki.net/pekka/monkey/#

Moodle
https://moodle.org

Museum of Modern Art (MoMA)
http://www.moma.org

National Archives
http://www.archives.gov/historical-docs/

National Geographic
http://www.nationalgeographic.com

National Geographic Kids
http://kids.nationalgeographic.com

National Library of Virtual Manipulatives
http://nlvm.usu.edu

netTrekker
http://www.nettrekker.com/us/

NOVA
http://www.pbs.org/wgbh/nova/

O_2 Learn
https://www.o2learn.co.uk

PBIS World
http://www.pbisworld.com/data-tracking/

PBS Kids
http://pbskids.org

PBS LearningMedia
http://www.pbslearningmedia.org

PBS TeacherLine
http://www.pbs.org/teacherline/

PBworks
http://pbworks.com

PhET Interactive Simulations
http://phet.colorado.edu

Piktochart
http://piktochart.com

Pinterest
http://www.pinterest.com

Poetry Foundation
http://www.poetryfoundation.org

Popplet app
https://itunes.apple.com/us/app/popplet/id374151636?mt=8

Prezi
http://prezi.com

Project Gutenberg
http://www.gutenberg.org

Puffin Books
http://www.puffin.co.uk

QuizStar
http://quizstar.4teachers.org

Random Name Selector Lite app
https://itunes.apple.com/us/app/random-name-selector-lite/
id589498393?mt=8

Ranger Rick
https://www.nwf.org/kids/ranger-rick.aspx

Reading A-Z
http://www.readinga-z.com/members/index.php

ReadWriteThink
http://www.readwritethink.org

Rhymer
> http://www.rhymer.com

RhymeZone
> http://www.rhymezone.com

Samsung Solve for Tomorrow
> http://www.samsung.com/us/solvefortomorrow/home.html

Scholastic
> http://www.scholastic.com

School Wide Information System (SWIS)
> https://www.pbisapps.org

Schoology
> https://www.schoology.com/home.php

SchoolRack
> http://www.schoolrack.com

ScoreItNow!
> https://www.dxrgroup.com/cgi-bin/scoreitnow/index.pl

Seeing Math
> http://seeingmath.concord.org/about_us.html

ShowMe
> http://www.showme.com

Singapore Math iPad apps
> http://singaporemathsource.com/resources/singapore-math-ipad-apps/

Skype
> http://www.skype.com

Socrative
> http://www.socrative.com

SoundingBoard
> http://www.ablenetinc.com/Assistive-Technology/Communication/
> SoundingBoard

Starfall
> http://www.starfall.com

Storia
http://store.scholastic.com/microsite/storia/about

Super Duper Publications
http://www.superduperinc.com

Teacher Blog It
http://www.teacherblogit.com

Teacher Tid Bytes
http://www.teachertidbytes.com

Teacher's Guide
http://www.theteachersguide.com

TeacherTube
http://www.teachertube.com

THE Journal
http://thejournal.com

TIME for Kids
http://www.timeforkids.com

Too Noisy Pro
http://toonoisyapp.com

Toontastic app
https://itunes.apple.com/us/app/toontastic-free/id404693282?mt=8

TourWrist
http://www.tourwrist.com

TumbleBooks
http://www.tumblebooks.com

University of Idaho Information Literacy
http://www.webpages.uidaho.edu/info_literacy/

VocabularySpellingCity
https://www.spellingcity.com

VoiceThread
http://voicethread.com

Voki
http://www.voki.com

Web 2.0 Guru
http://web20guru.com

WebQuest
http://webquest.org

Wikispaces
http://www.wikispaces.com

Wordle
http://www.wordle.net

WritingFix
http://writingfix.com

Yoursphere
https://yoursphere.com/welcome

YouTube
http://www.youtube.com

Zoho Wiki
https://www.zoho.com/wiki/

Software

Cabri 3D
http://www.cabri.com/cabri-3d.html

iMovie
http://www.apple.com/ios/imovie

Inspiration
http://www.inspiration.com

Kidspiration
http://www.inspiration.com/Kidspiration

Microsoft Office for PC
http://www.microsoftstore.com

Microsoft Photo Story
http://microsoft-photo-story.en.softonic.com

Movie Maker
http://windows.microsoft.com

Oregon Trail by The Learning Company
http://www.oregontrail.com/hmh/site/oregontrail/

Rosetta Stone
http://www.rosettastone.com

Texts

Dahl, Roald. 1964. *Charlie and the Chocolate Factory.* New York: Alfred A. Knopf.

White, E. B. 1952. *Charlotte's Web.* New York: Harper & Row Publishers.

References Cited

Ainsworth, Larry. 2006. "Common Formative Assessments: The Centerpiece of an Integrated Standards-Based Assessment System." In *Ahead of the Curve: The Power of Assessment to Transform Teaching and Learning*, edited by Douglas Reeves, 79–102. Bloomington, IN: Solution Tree.

American Library Association, The. 2013. "Introduction to Information Literacy." http://www.ala.org/acrl/issues/infolit/overview/intro.

Arora, Keerti. 2013. "Social Media in Education: Pros and Cons." *EdTechReview.* http://edtechreview.in/e-learning/268-socia-media-in-education-pros-cons.

Berthiaume, Gayle. 2013. "100 Ways to Use Digital Cameras." Scholastic. http://www.scholastic.com/teachers/lesson-plan/100-ways-use-digital-cameras.

Bidwell, Allie. 2013. "How Virtual Games Can Help Struggling Students Learn." *U.S. News & World Report.* http://www.usnews.com/news/articles/2013/11/26/how-virtual-games-can-help-struggling-students-learn.

Blazer, Christie. 2008. "Improving the Classroom Environment: Classroom Amplification Systems." LightSPEED Technologies, Inc.

Bowen, Tim. 2013. "Teaching Approaches: Total Physical Response." One Stop English; Macmillan English Campus. Accessed November 18. http://www.onestopenglish.com/support/methodology/teaching-approaches/teaching-approaches-total-physical-response/146503.article.

Brozek, Elizabeth, and Debra Duckworth. 2011. "Supporting English Language Learners Through Technology." *Educator's Voice* 4: 10–15. https://www.nysut.org/~/media/Files/NYSUT/Resources/2011/March/Educators%20Voice%204%20Technology/edvoiceIV_ch2.pdf.

Cattie, Christopher, and Kris van Riper. 2012. "Collaboration's Role in the New Work Environment." FCW: The Business of Federal Technology. Accessed July 29, 2013. http://fcw.com/articles/2012/12/07/collaboration-in-agency-environments.aspx.

Cheung, Alan, and Robert E. Slavin. 2012. *"The Effectiveness of Educational Technology Applications for Enhancing Reading Achievement in K–12 Classrooms: A Meta-Analysis."* Baltimore, MD: Johns Hopkins University, Center for Research and Reform in Education.

Childress, Gregory. 2014. "Student of the Month: Creative Studies Sophomore Wise Beyond Years." *The Herald Sun.* http://www.heraldsun.com/news/showcase/x571857963/Student-of-the-Month-Creative-Studies-sophomore-wise-beyond-years.

Clark, Carol. 2010. "Why Teach Poetry?" Cambridge, MA: Educational Publishing Services, Inc.

Clark, Kim. 2008. "Professors Use Technology to Fight Student Cheating." *U.S. News and World Report.*

CompTIA. 2011. "Making the Grade: Technology Helps Boost Student Performance, Staff Productivity in Nation's Schools, New CompTIA Study Finds," press release. http://www.comptia.org/about-us/newsroom/press-releases/11-06-28/Making_the_Grade_Technology_Helps_Boosts_Student_Performance_Staff_Productivity_in_Nation's_Schools_New_CompTIA_Study_Finds.aspx.

Conklin, Wendy. 2012. *Higher-Order Thinking Skills to Develop 21st Century Learners.* Huntington Beach, CA: Shell Education.

Cornell University Center for Teaching Excellence. 2014. "Collaborative Learning: Group Work." http://www.cte.cornell.edu/teaching-ideas/engaging-students/collaborative-learning.html.

Cuban, Larry. 2013. "Technologies I Used in My Classroom in the 1950s: Recapturing How I Taught A Half-Century Ago." http://larrycuban. wordpress.com/2013/09/06/technologies-i-used-in-my-classroom-in-the-1950s-recapturing-how-i-taught-a-half-century-ago/.

Curriculum21. 2014. "What Is Curriculum Mapping?" http://www. curriculum21.com/pd/curriculum-mapping/mapping-defined/.

Dalton, Bridget. 2008. "Integrating Language, Culture, and Technology to Achieve New Literacies for All." In *Technology-Mediated Learning Environments for Young English Learners,* edited by L. Leann Parker. New York, NY: Lawrence Erlbaum Associates.

Darling-Hammond, Linda. 2010. *The Flat World And Education: How America's Commitment To Equity Will Determine Our Future.* New York, NY: Teacher's College Press.

Davis, Michelle R. 2008. "Exergaming Blends Tech and Exercise in Gym Classes." *Education Week*. http://www.edweek.org/dd/ articles/2008/04/30/04physed2_web.h01.html.

Department for Education. 2013. "Digital Technology in Schools." http:// webarchive.nationalarchives.gov.uk/20130802141748/https://www. education.gov.uk/schools/teachingandlearning/curriculum/a00201823/ digital-technology-in-schools.

Digregorio, Peter, and Karen Sobel-Lojeski. 2009–2010. "The Effects of Interactive Whiteboards (IWBs) on Student Performance and Learning: A Literature Review." *Journal of Educational Technology Systems* 38 (3): 255–312.

Doran, George, Arthur Miller, and James Cunningham. 1981. "There's a S.M.A.R.T. Way to Write Management's Goals and Objectives." *Management Review* 70 (11): 35–36.

DuFour, Richard. 2004. "What Is a Professional Learning Community?" *Educational Leadership* 61 (8): 6–11.

Dunn, Jeff. 2011. "The Evolution of Classroom Technology." Edudemic. http://www.edudemic.com/classroom-technology/.

Dymoke, Susan. 2008. "Wireless Keyboards And Mice: Could They Enhance Teaching And Learning In The Secondary English Classroom?" *English in Education 39* (3): 62–67.

East Windsor Public School District. 2014. "Information Technology." Accessed October 2. http://www.eastwindsork12.org/pages/East_ Windsor_SD/Information_Technology.

Editorial Projects in Education Research Center. 2011. "Technology in Education." *Education Week*. http://www.edweek.org/ew/issues/ technology-in-education/.

Education World. 2014. "Teachers Teaching Teachers: Professional Development That Works." Accessed October 2. http://www. educationworld.com/a_admin/admin/admin459.shtml.

Educational Technology Network. 2009. "Document Cameras in the Classroom." http://www.edtechnetwork.com/document_cameras.html.

Educational Testing Service. 2013. "Automated Scoring and Natural Language Processing." Accessed July 25. http://www.ets.org/research/ topics/as_nlp/.

Edutopia. 2007. "The Sky's the Limit: Kids' Top Tools for the Classroom." http://www.edutopia.org/student-opinions-classroom-technology-tools.

Emerson, Ralph Waldo. 2013. Move Me Quotes. Accessed July 21. http:// www.movemequotes.com/tag/lead-by-example/.

Emmer, Edmund, Edward Sabornie, Carolyn M. Evertson, and Carol S. Weinstein, eds. 2006. *Handbook of Classroom Management: Research, Practice, and Contemporary Issues*. New York, NY: Routledge.

Encomium. 2014. "Interactive Test Prep for the TOEFL." http://www. encomiuminteractive.com/exams/products_detail.asp?egid=3.

Evertson, Carolyn M., and Carol S. Weinstein. 2006. *Handbook of Classroom Management: Research, Practice, and Contemporary Issues*. Malwah, NJ: Lawrence Erlbaum Associates.

Farwell, Terry. 2012. "Visual, Auditory, Kinesthetic Learners." *Family Education*. School and Learning section, accessed 9/4/14 from http://school.familyeducation.com/intelligence/teaching-methods/38519.html.

Fasimpaur, Karen. 2003. "Using eBooks in Education." *Southeast Initiatives Regional Technology in Education Consortium Newswire* 6 (1): 12–13.

Ferdig, Richard E., and Kaye D. Trammell. 2004. "Content Delivery In The Blogosphere." *The Journal Online.* http://defiant.corban.edu/jjohnson/Pages/Teaching/BloggingBlogosphere.pdf.

Finkel, Ed. 2012. "Flipping the Script in K12." http://www.districtadministration.com/article/flipping-script-k12.

Fisher, Douglas, and Nancy Frey. 2011. *Engaging the Adolescent Learner: Using Video and Film in the Classroom.* Newark, DE: International Reading Association.

Fitzgerald, Thomas. 2012. "Bringing Up an E-Reader." *New York Times.* http://www.nytimes.com/2012/03/29/technology/personaltech/bringing-up-a-young-reader-on-e-books.html?_r=0.

Frederick, Wayne C., and Herbert J. Klausmeier. 1969. "A Schema for Testing the Level of Cognitive Mastery." Madison, WI: Wisconsin Center for Education Research. http://www.readingeducator.com/strategies/frayer.htm.

Goodwin, Bryan, and Kirsten Miller. 2013. "Research Says / Evidence on Flipped Classrooms Is Still Coming." *Educational Leadership* 70 (6): 78–80.

Grady, Marilyn L. 2011. *Leading the Technology-Powered School.* Thousand Oaks, CA: Corwin Press.

Griffith, Lorraine W., and Timothy Rasinski. 2004. "A Focus on Fluency: How One Teacher Incorporated Fluency with Her Reading Curriculum." *The Reading Teacher* 58 (2): 126–133.

Grinager, Heather. 2006. "How Education Technology Leads to Improved Student Achievement." *National Conference of State Legislatures: Education Issues.* http://www.ncsl.org/portals/1/documents/educ/item013161.pdf.

Grunwald Associates, LLC. 2013. "Living and Learning with Mobile Devices: What Parents Think About Mobile Devices for Early Childhood and K–12 Learning." http://grunwald.com/pdfs/ Grunwald%20Mobile%20Study%20public%20report.pdf.

Guernsey, Lisa, and Sara Mead. 2014. "Transforming Education in the Primary Years." University of Texas at Dallas. Accessed October 2. http://www.pikeschool.org/uploaded/Research_Articles/ Transforming_Education_in_the_Primary_Years.pdf.

Harmon, Janis M., Karen D. Wood, Wanda B. Hedrick, and Jean Vintinner. 2009. "Interactive Word Walls: More Than Just Reading the Writing on the Walls." *Journal of Adolescent & Adult Literacy* 52 (5): 398–408.

Harvey, Stephanie, and Anne Goudvis. 2007. *Strategies That Work*. 2nd ed. Portland, ME: Stenhouse Publishers, Inc.

Hasselbring, Ted S., and Candyce H. Williams Glaser. 2000. "Use of Computer Technology to Help Students with Special Needs." *The Future of Children: Children and Computer Technology* 10 (2): 102–122.

Hawkins, Jan. 1997. "The World at Your Fingertips." In *Live & Learn*, edited by Patty Burness and William Snider, 213–215. Nicasio, CA: The George Lucas Educational Foundation.

Hayes Jacobs, Heidi. 2010. *Curriculum 21: Essential Education for a Changing World*. Alexandria, VA: Association for Supervision and Curriculum Development.

Henderson, Anne T., and Karen L. Mapp. 2002. "A New Wave of Evidence: The Impact of School, Family, and Community Connections on Student Achievement." Southwest Educational Development Laboratory (SEDL) National Center for Family and Community. Accessed May 6, 2014. http://www.sedl.org/connections/resources/ evidence.pdf.

Hetzroni, Orit E., and Betty Shrieber. 2004. "Word Processing as an Assistive Technology Tool for Enhancing Academic Outcome of Students with Writing Disabilities in the General Classroom." *Journal of Learning Disabilities* 37 (2): 143–154.

Hutton, Shannon. 2013. "Helping Visual Learners Succeed" *Education*. http://www.education.com/magazine/article/Helping_Visual_ Learners/.

Hutton, Thaashida L. 2008. "Three Tiers of Vocabulary and Education." Super Duper Handy Handouts No. 182. Super Duper Publications, Inc. http://www.superduperinc.com/handouts/handout.aspx.

International Society for Technology in Education (ISTE). 2012. "ISTE Standards." Washington D.C.: ISTE http://www.iste.org/standards.

International Technology Education Association (ITEA). 2009. "The Overlooked STEM Imperatives: Technology and Engineering, K–12 Education." Reston, VA: ITEA.

Intervention Central. 2014. "How To: Teach Students to Change Behaviors Through Self-Monitoring." Accessed October 2. http://www. interventioncentral.org/self_management_self_monitoring.

Kopp, Kathleen. 2013. *Using Interactive Whiteboards in the Classroom*. Huntington Beach, CA: Shell Education.

Kuntz, Brad. 2012. "Engage Students by Embracing Technology: In the Classroom with Brad Kuntz." *Education Update* 54 (6).

Kurzweil Educational Systems. 2004. "Using Technology as a Solution for English Language Learners in Higher Education." http://www. kurzweiledu.com/files/kurzweil–3000–ell–higher–ed.pdf.

Larmer, John, and John R. Mergendoller. 2010. "Seven Essentials for Project-Based Learning." *Educational Leadership* 68 (1): 34–37.

Lenhart, Amanda, Sousan Arafeh, Aaron Smith, and Alexandra Macgill. 2008. "Writing, Technology, and Teens." Pew Research Internet Project http://www.pewinternet.org/2008/04/24/writing-technology- and-teens/.

Levin, Barbara B., and Lynne Schrum. 2013. "Technology-Rich Schools Up Close." *Educational Leadership* 70 (6): 51–55.

Lindberg, Jill, Michele Flasch Ziegler, and Lisa Barczyk. 2009. *Common-Sense Classroom Management: Techniques for Working with Students with Disabilities*. Thousand Oaks, CA: Corwin Press.

Linder, Sandra M. 2012. "Interactive Whiteboards in Early Childhood Mathematics: Strategies for Effective Implementation in Pre-K–Grade 3." *Young Children* 67 (3): 26–32, 34–35.

MacArthur, Charles, Steve Graham, and Jill Fitzgerald, ed. 2006. *Handbook of Writing Research*. New York, NY: The Guilford Press.

MacArthur Foundation. 2011. "Exploring Digital Media and Learning." Accessed September 1, 2013. http://www.macfound.org/media/article_pdfs/DML_BUFF_MARCH_2011.PDF.

March, Tom. 2003. "The Learning Power of WebQuests." *Educational Leadership* 61 (4): 42–47.

Marzano, Robert J., Debra Pickering, and Jane E. Pollock. 2001. *Classroom Instruction that Works: Research-based Strategies for Increasing Student Achievement*. Alexandria, VA: Association for Supervision and Curriculum Development.

Marzano, Robert J. 2009. "Teaching with Interactive Whiteboards." *Educational Leadership* 67 (3): 80–82.

Marzano, Robert J. 2010. "The Art and Science of Teaching: Using Games to Enhance Student Achievement." *Educational Leadership* 67 (5): 71–72.

Marzano, Robert J., and Mark Haystead. 2010. "Final Report: A Second Year Evaluation Study of Promethean ActivClassroom." Marzano Research Laboratory. http://www.prometheanworld.com/rx_content/files/PDF/Marzano2ndYearStudyofPrometheanActivClassroom-169662.pdf.

McTighe, Jay, and Ken O'Connor. 2005."Seven Practices for Effective Learning." *Educational Leadership* 63 (3): 10-17. http://www.ascd.org/publications/educational-leadership/nov05/vol63/num03/Seven-Practices-for-Effective-Learning.aspx.

Means, Barbara, Yukie Toyama, Robert Murphy, Marianne Bakia, and Karla Jones. 2009. "*Evaluation of Evidence-based Practices in Online Learning: A Meta-analysis and Review of Online Learning Studies.*" Washington, DC: U.S. Department of Education, Office of Planning, Evaluation and Policy Development.

Merriam–Webster Online, s.v. "routine." 2014. Acessed October 2. http://www.merriam–webster.com/dictionary/routine

Mind Tool. 2014. "How Your Learning Style Affects Your Use of Mnemonics." Accessed October 1. http://www.mindtools.com/mnemlstylo.htm.

Moore Kneas, Kimberly, and Bruce D. Perry. 2014. "Using Technology in the Early Childhood Classroom." *Scholastic.* Accessed October 1. http://teacher.scholastic.com/professional/bruceperry/using_technology.htm.

Morgan, Michael. 2008. "More Productive Use of Technology in the ESL/EFL Classroom." *The Internet TESOL Journal* 14 (7).

Nagel, David. 2014. "6 Shifts in Education Driven by Technology." *The Journal.* http://thejournal.com/articles/2014/05/21/6-shifts-in-education-driven-by-technology.aspx.

National Center for Education Statistics. 2014. "Create a Graph." Kids! Zone. Accessed October 2. http://nces.ed.gov/nceskids/createagraph/.

National Governors Association (NGA) Center for Best Practices and Council of Chief State School Officers (CCSSO). 2010. "Common Core State Standards: English Language Arts Standards." Washington, DC: National Governors Association Center for Best Practices, Council of Chief State School Officers. http://www.corestandards.org.

National Governors Association (NGA) Center for Best Practices and Council of Chief State School Officers (CCSSO). 2010. "Common Core State Standards: Speaking and Listening." Washington, DC: National Governors Association Center for Best Practices, Council of Chief State School Officers. http://www.corestandards.org.

National Mathematics Advisory Panel. 2008. "Foundations for Success: The Final Report of National Mathematics Advisory Panel." Jessup, MD: U.S. Department of Education.

National Science Teachers Association. 2010. "Teaching Science and Technology in the Context of Societal and Personal Issues." http://www.nsta.org/docs/PositionStatement_TeachingScienceAndTechnology.pdf.

Ohio Department of Education. 2003. "Ohio's 2003 Academic Content Standards in Technology." http://education.ohio.gov/Topics/Academic-Content-Standards/Technology/Ohio-s-2003-Academic-Content-Standards-in-Technolo.

Oregon Department of Education. 2013. "Educational Technology–Standards." Accessed August 10. http://www.ode.state.or.us/search/page/?id=1880.

Partnership for 21st Century Skills. 2013. "A Vision for 21st Century Citizenship." Accessed July 28. http://www.p21.org/our-work/citizenship.

Pikulski, John J., and David J. Chard. 2005. "Fluency: Bridge Between Decoding and Reading Comprehension." *The Reading Teacher 58* (6): 510–519.

Pinnell, Gay Su, and Irene C. Fountas. 2008. *The Continuum of Literacy Learning, K–8: Behaviors and Understandings to Notice, Teach, and Support*. Portsmouth, NH: Heinemann.

Pitler, Howard, Elizabeth R. Hubbell, Matt Kuhn, and Kim Malenoski. 2007. *Using Technology with Classroom Instruction That Works*. Alexandria, VA: Association for Supervision and Curriculum Development.

Purcell, Kristen, Judy Buchanan, and Linda Friedrich. 2013. "The Impact of Digital Tools on Student Writing and How Writing is Taught in Schools." Pew Research Internet Project. http://www.pewinternet.org/2013/07/16/the-impact-of-digital-tools-on-student-writing-and-how-writing-is-taught-in-schools/.

Richardson, Will. 2010. *Blogs, Wikis, Podcasts, and Other Powerful Web Tools for Classrooms.* Thousand Oaks, CA: Corwin.

Riconscente, Michelle. 2013. "Motion Math in Class." *Game Desk.* http://gamedesk.org/project/motion-math-in-class/.

Rose, David. 2004. "The Role of Technology in the Guided Reading Classroom." Scholastic Professional Paper, Scholastic, Inc. http://teacher.scholastic.com/products/authors/pdfs/WW_GR_prof_paper.pdf.

Roskos, Kathleen, Karen Burstein, Yi Shang, and Emily Gray. 2014. "Young Children's Engagement with eBooks at School: Does Device Matter?" SAGE Open. http://sgo.sagepub.com/content/4/1/2158244013517244.

Rubenstein, Grace. 2008. "The DNA of Learning: Teens Tackle Animal Poaching Through Genetics." *Edutopia.* http://www.edutopia.org/high-tech-high-biotech-video.

Salies, Tania Gastao. 2002. "Simulations/Gaming in the EAP Writing Class: Benefits and Drawbacks." *Simulation & Gaming* 33 (3): 316–329.

Sams, Aaron, and Jonathan Bergmann. 2013. *Flip Your Classroom.* Washington, DC: International Society for Technology in Education.

Sawchuk, Stephen. 2009. "The Online Option." *Education Week.* http://www.edweek.org/tsb/articles/2009/10/01/01online.h03.html.

Schaffhauser, Dian. 2013. "Online Testing." *THE Journal* 40 (7): 5–11. http://thejournal.realviewdigital.com/?iid=88504#folio=1.

Scheie, Emily. 2014. "Teachers Track Student Behavior with Swipes and Clicks." *World.* http://www.worldmag.com/2014/08/teachers_track_student_behavior_with_swipes_and_clicks.

Schenk, David. 1997. *Data Smog.* New York, NY: Harper Collins Publishing.

Scherer, Marge. 2012. "The Challenges of Supporting New Teachers: A Conversation with Linda Darling-Hammond." *Educational Leadership* 69 (8): 18–23.

Schwab Foundation for Learning. 2000. "Assistive Technology for Children with Learning Difficulties." In *Bridges to Reading*, 2nd ed. San Mateo, CA: Schwab Foundation for Learning.

Sesame Street. 2010. "There's an App for That." Accessed September 15, 2013. http://www.youtube.com/watch?v=EhkxDIr0y2U.

Shanahan, Timothy, Douglas Fisher, and Nancy Frey. 2012. "The Challenge of Challenging Text." *Educational Leadership* 69 (6): 58–62.

Shin, Namsoo, LeeAnn M. Sutherland, Cathleen A. Norris, and Elliot Soloway. 2012. "Effects of Game Technology on Elementary Student Learning in Mathematics." *British Journal of Educational Technology* 43 (4): 540–560.

Simkins, Michael, Karen Cole, Fern Tavalin, and Barbara Means. 2002. *Increasing Student Learning through Multimedia Projects*. Alexandria, VA: Association for Supervision and Curriculum Development.

Snyder, Tom. 2014. "The Graph Club 2.0." Tom Snyder Productions. Accessed October 2. http://www.journeyed.com/item/Tom+Snyder/ The+Graph+Club/100960266.

Stokes, Audrey. 2011. "Expert Article: Making the Case for Teaching with New Media." *Common Sense Education* https://www. commonsensemedia.org/educators/blog/expert-article-making-the-case-for-teaching-with-new-media.

Tamim, Rana M., Robert M. Bernard, Eugene Borokhovski, Philip C. Arami, and Richard F. Schmid. 2011. "What Forty Years of Research Says About the Impact of Technology on Learning: A Second-order Meta-Analysis and Validation Study." *Review of Educational Research 81* (1): 4–28.

TeachThought. 2012. "10 Ideas for Using Technology to Teach Writing." http://www.teachthought.com/technology/10-ideas-for-using-technology-to-teach-writing/.

Tomlinson, Carol Ann. 2005. "Differentiating Instruction: Why Bother?" *Middle Ground* 9 (1): 12–14.

Topol, Barry, John Olson, and Ed Roeber. 2011. *The Cost of New Higher Quality Assessments: A Comprehensive Analysis of the Potential Costs for Future State Assessments.* Palo Alto, CA: Stanford.

Tucker, Bill. 2009. "The Next Generation of Testing." *Educational Leadership* 67 (3): 48–53.

Tuzun, Hakan, Meryem Yilmaz-Soylu, Turkan Karakus, Yavuz Inal, and Gonca Kizilkaya. 2009. "The Effects of Computer Games on Primary School Students' Achievement and Motivation in Geography Learning." *Computers & Education* 52 (1): 68–77.

Ullman, Ellen. 2011. "How To Plan Effective Lessons." *ASCD* 53 (10).

United States Census Bureau. 2013. "Computer and Internet Use in the United States, 2011." Accessed July 28, 2013 http://www.census.gov/hhes/computer/publications/2011.html.

University of Idaho. 2014. "Information Literacy." http://www.webpages.uidaho.edu/info_literacy/.

University of Texas at Austin. 2014. "Author Studies Research Guide." Accessed September 11. http://www.lib.utexas.edu/subject/education/author-studies.

U.S. Department of Education. 2008. "The Basics—Helping Your Child Succeed in School." http://www2.ed.gov/parents/academic/help/succeed/part4.html.

U.S. Department of Education. 2010. "How People Need to Learn." http://www.ed.gov/technology/draft-netp-2010/how-people-need-to-learn.

U.S. Department of Education. 2010. "Transforming American Education: Learning Powered by Technology, National Education Technology Plan, 2010." http://tech.ed.gov/wp-content/uploads/2013/10/netp2010.pdf#page=35.

U.S. Department of Education. 2014. "Use of Technology in Teaching and Learning." Accessed October 2. http://www.ed.gov/oii-news/use-technology-teaching-and-learning.

Vanderbilt University. 2014. "Bloom's Taxonomy." http://cft.vanderbilt.edu/guides-sub-pages/blooms-taxonomy/.

Vasinda, Sheri, and Julie McLeod. 2011. "Extending Readers Theatre: A Powerful and Purposeful Match with Podcasting." *The Reading Teacher* 64: 486–497. http://www.readingrockets.org/article/52140/.

Vincent-Lancrin, Stéphan. 2013. "Creativity in Schools: What Countries Do (or Could Do)." The Organisation for Economic Co-operation and Development (OECD). http://oecdeducationtoday.blogspot.com/2013/01/creativity-in-schools-what-countries-do.html.

Wait, Brittany. 2013. "Google Teacher Academy Accepts Deer Park High School Teacher Christopher Kauter." *Newsday*.

Wang, Margaret, Geneva D. Haertel, and Herbert J. Walberg. 1993. "Toward a Knowledge Base for School Learning." *Review of Educational Research 63* (3): 249–294.

Waxman, Olivia B. 2012. "How Teachers Use Skype in the Classroom." *TIME*. http://techland.time.com/2012/11/28/how-teachers-use-skype-in-the-classroom/.

WebQuest. 2007. http://webquest.org.

Wedig, Timothy. 2010. "Getting the Most from Classroom Simulations: Strategies for Maximizing Learning Outcomes." *PS, Political Science and Politics,* July: 547–555.

Wei, Ruth Chung, Alethea Andree, and Linda Darling-Hammond. 2009. "How Nations Invest in Teachers." *Educational Leadership 66* (5): 28–33.

Weis, June. 2003. "Information Literacy: One of the New 21st Century Learning Skills." *Southeast Initiatives Regional Technology in Education Consortium Newswire* 6 (1): 17–22 . http://education.ucf.edu/mirc/Research/SEIRTEC%20-%20Technology%20Reading%20Instruction.pdf. WHEC-TV. 2013. "Students and Staff Use Legos to Recreate a Natural Disaster Response." http://www.whec.com/news/stories/S3160069.shtml?cat=565.